DEATH IN GRIMSBY
50 years following
Brighton & Hove Albion

Also by Nic Outterside
The Adventures of Nathan Sunnybank
The Hill - Songs and Poems of Darkness and Light
Another Hill – Songs and Poems of Love and Theft
Asian Voices
Blood in the Cracks
Luminance - Words for a World Gone Wrong

About the author
Nic Outterside was an award-winning newspaper journalist
and editor for 28 years and currently is the proprietor of
Time is an Ocean, the book publishing arm of **write***ahead*.
Death in Grimsby is his seventh paperback book.

DEATH IN GRIMSBY
50 years following
Brighton & Hove Albion

Nic Outterside

Time is an Ocean Publications

Time is an Ocean Publications
An Imprint of **write**_ahead_
Lonsdale Road
Wolverhampton, WV3 0DY

First Printed Edition written and published
by **Time is an Ocean Publications 2019**
Text copyright © **Nic Outterside, 2019**
The right of Nic Outterside to be identified as the author of
this work has been asserted by him, in accordance with the
Copyright, Designs and Patents Act 1988.
The front cover artwork is taken from an original
photograph by **Nigel Hardy**.
The back cover is a photograph of an
original stained glass by **Mark Baird**.
All images within this book are copyright
Time is an Ocean except where
the individual copyright of the owners are accredited.

DEDICATION

For David Knott, who took me to my first
Brighton and Hove Albion game.
Also for Alan Willard, Ian Hine, Ash Bradley and
Janice Merritt who through encouragement and
assistance made this book possible.
And to Gill Outterside for her patience and skill in
proofing the entire manuscript.
But most of all for Kit Napier now ghosting past
opposition defences in the Albion's Field of Dreams.

CONTENTS

Introduction

The one thing I have learned as I have got older is that this life we are each given is very short.

When we die we can only hope to leave behind a good legacy. But while we are here, we need a passion or two to give our lives some meaning. I have three: my family, the music of Bob Dylan, and Brighton and Hove Albion FC.

At the time of writing, I have been following my home town football club for a full 52 years and witnessed many highs and lows, and thankfully very few periods of mid-table mediocrity.

Like a fan of whatever club you support, whether that be Arsenal, Accrington Stanley, Aston Villa or Alloa Athletic, football is tribal, loyal, consuming and most of all, passionate.

My own passion for Brighton and Hove Albion was conceived on a sunny Saturday afternoon in September 1967 when I was just 11 years old, as I stood wide-eyed at the front of the North Stand of the Goldstone Ground watching these huge men battle for a crisp, white ball on the green turf before me.

The gestation developed during my adolescence despite my father moving the whole family to Hertfordshire less than a year later.

My passion was then nurtured by my first night game against Portsmouth in 1969, by trips to weird and wonderful places such as Luton, Halifax, Tranmere and Walsall, and even by whole weekends at Barrow and Southport.

Moving away to college in West Yorkshire in 1974 allowed the passion to bloom. To the best of my knowledge, I was one of only three people at Huddersfield Polytechnic who were staunch Brighton and Hove Albion supporters… this assertion is based purely on the fact that whenever I shouted out *"Seagulls"* in the Student Union bar only two others would answer!

The so-called adult years that followed tested my passion many times. Supporting my club from northern Scotland, Tyneside, Yorkshire, Shropshire and North Wales failed to dim a love that had grown inside and become part of the person I am now.

The triumph at St James' Park in 1979, a Wembley FA Cup Final in 1983, the draw against Hereford in 1997 and promotion to the

1

Premier League in 2017 are as vital to that desire as the 8-2 home defeat to Bristol Rovers in 1973, being thumped 4-1 in the League Cup by Barnsley in 1981, losing the Goldstone Ground in 1997 and the wet and miserable years at Gillingham and the Withdean.

And one added bonus of being a Brighton and Hove Albion fanatic is making so many football friends along the way - not only among fellow fans, but also those rivals from other clubs, notably Blackpool, Cambridge United, Celtic, Newcastle United, Stranraer, Wolves and Wrexham.

And that brings me to the book you are holding in front of you.

I have been a professional writer, journalist and newspaper editor for more than 34 years. In recent years I have also written and published six books – including one on Bob Dylan. But for some strange reason I had avoided writing about the football club I have followed for so long. It wasn't even on my radar, far less on any publishing schedule.

Then out of the blue (or maybe out of the blue and white) in October 2018, an old Albion friend, Alan Willard, who runs a Facebook group aptly named *The Goldstone Ground* suggested I add my own book to his huge library of all things Brighton and Hove Albion.

So with a spark of an idea in my head, I sketched out a framework and wrote the first piece in November. Chapters started to roll together, and by April 2019 *Death in Grimsby* was completed. It is fundamentally a personal memoir of short stories, told chronologically, over the first 50 years of following my passion.

It starts with my first game at the Goldstone in September 1967 and finishes with the match against Wolves at Molineux in April 2017, when we all but mathematically secured promotion to the Premier League.

Each chapter is a separate tale related to 21 different games and events over those years. These are knitted together with many personal recollections such as meeting Ernie Wise in Leeds before our match in 1980, interviewing Paul Gascoigne in 1995, trying to explain the Foot and Mouth funeral pyres to my young daughters before our game against Carlisle United in 2001 and being hospitalised with hypothermia after our freezing, rain sodden match at Grimsby in 2004.

My wife Gill's first Albion game was at Port Vale in 2014. It remains a treasured memory for many reasons, not least her immediately embracing the Albion chants, and her total revulsion at the food on offer at the refreshment outlets. So each chapter is tailgated with a piece about the unique foodstuff available at our many football grounds around the country. From Black Pudding Muffins at Bury to Butter Pie at Preston and Stottie and Pease Pudding at Newcastle, I ate them all!

This book would not have been possible without the inspiration, encouragement and assistance from the aforesaid Mr Willard, my wife, and long-time Albion friends: Ian Hine, the librarian of the biggest collection of BHAFC programmes on the planet; the remarkable die-hard Janice Merritt, who has been to more Albion games than I can count; and the unbridled enthusiasm of *Asda Trolley Monkey* and fellow Albion fanatic Ash Bradley.

I must also thank the many other Albion fans who have provided images for this book – they are all acknowledged and thanked individually and at the back.

As the late Roy Chuter once said: *"The beauty of football isn't just the 90 minutes you see – it is the social side of it. It's your family, it's your friends."* UTA forever.

Nic Outterside (2019)

Chapter One

Popping my Cherry Against Bury
The Goldstone Ground
2 September 1967

The Brighton and Hove Albion squad 1967/68   © The Argus

Every Brighton and Hove Albion story has a beginning, and this is mine... pure and simple, pumped full of childhood naivety and the roots of a passion which would last a lifetime.
I spent six idyllic early years of my life with my family in a spacious bungalow in the new village of Mile Oak nestled on the South Downs, just east of Hove.

These were my growing up and playing-till-the-sun-went-down years.

They were blissfully happy in their innocence and the summers were never ending. The warmth of those years will always stay with me, locked into my memories like scenes from Harper Lee's *To Kill a Mockingbird*.

My mother gave me freedom to roam on the wide open hills that surrounded us, and play at soldiers, cowboys, space explorers or whatever fancy captured our childish imaginations.

I had three close friends and we rarely played indoors. Even when the weather was wet, we ventured forth either as a group or in pairs into our natural playground.

I guess in hindsight our mothers harboured few fears for our safety, as long as we were back for lunch and tea… and definitely before it got dark.

So nothing stopped us exploring a disused isolation hospital, a chalk quarry, a tumbledown "witch's cottage" or a former army training ground, from where I brought home a live hand grenade… but that's another story for another book!

But better than all of that was playing football in the road outside our homes – taking turns to run after the ball if it tailed away down the steep hill of Oakdene Crescent onto Mile Oak Road.

It was real time adventure and unbridled innocent fun for young boys.

But the summer of 1967 was also time to do a little growing up.

I had just passed my 11+ Exam – much to my parents' delight – and in September was set to enter Hove County Grammar School for Boys… an Edwardian red brick institution of blazers, gowns, Latin detentions, cold showers and six whacks of the cane for bad behaviour.

I shuddered at the thought of change… but also grinned widely with anticipation.

The school was four miles away from my home, in Holmes Avenue, and close to somewhere which had captured my childish imagination for the previous two years: The Goldstone Ground… home to the famous (at least locally) Brighton and Hove Albion.

It was a place I had only ever seen from the top deck of the local Number 26 bus on the Old Shoreham Road, during occasional shopping trips into Brighton.

Until that point in time I had only followed this football team through the back pages of the Brighton *Argus* daily newspaper or by enacting matches with my beloved blue and white Brighton and Hove Albion *Subbuteo* table football team.

Lucy was in the Sky with Diamonds, but at the end of the so-called *Summer of Love* I was about to begin a love affair that would give me greater highs than any acid trip.

So there I was, a wide-eyed 11-year-old kid praying that one day my father – who loved golf and hated soccer - might one day take me to the Goldstone Ground to watch a game.

He wouldn't, and sadly never did, despite the fact that his own father was a Newcastle United fanatic. But all that changed on the weekend before I was due to start at the grammar school. My neighbour David Knott was 32, and as an Albion nut, seemed cursed to have a daughter who hated football. And on that late summer day my Christmas wish suddenly came true.

Mum broke the news: *"Julie's husband asked whether you would like to go to a football match with him?"*

I couldn't get the words: *"Yes please"* out of my mouth either quicker or louder than if someone had asked: *"Would you like a space rocket trip to Mars?"*

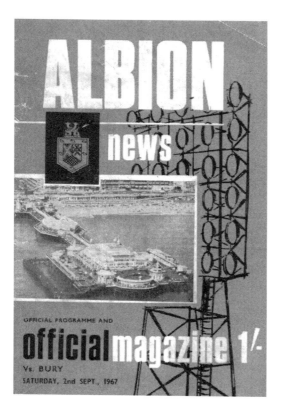

And at that moment I became David's Saturday surrogate son, at least for the purposes of having someone to take to matches at the Goldstone Ground.

So my first Albion game was on a bright and sunny Saturday (2nd September 1967) and it was a real trip into dreamland as not only did I witness "my team" playing right in front of me, but I also witnessed a 1-0 home win against Bury in front of a bustling 13,413 crowd.

I stood with David near the front right of the North Stand and watched in awe as these 22 huge men battled it out with a gleaming white ball on the sun-kissed grass.

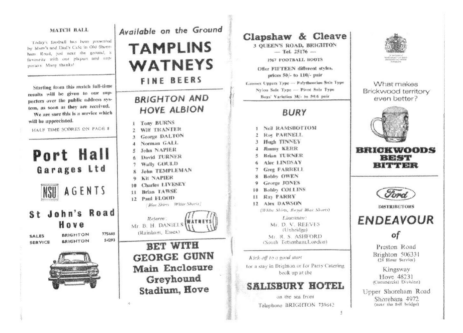

I soaked it all in, including the fact – relayed to me by David - that Bury were captained by Scottish international Bobby Collins, who was hard in the tackle and ran the show from midfield... at least until we scored.

Our scorer was a tousle-haired inside forward named Kit Napier. He became my immediate hero, and along with Brylcreem-blond crowd favourite Charlie Livesey, he remains a personal Albion legend.

Others in our team that day were the solid Norman Gall, the towering John Napier (no relation to Kit), Dave Turner, George Dalton, the young midfield dynamo John Templeman and two wily wingers Wally Gould and Brian "Tiger" Tawse, who would match Knockaert and Izquierdo for trickery, but maybe not fitness, particularly if they had a cigarette or two at half time.

My first Albion hero, the legend, the wizard, the goal scorer that will always be Kit Napier © The Argus

But for me Kit Napier had everything… fleet footed, devastatingly fast, a provider and a scorer, a genius at riding tackles and ghosting past opposition defences in one move.

He could also deliver amazing in-swinging corners from the right and scored directly from one against Bury in December 1969. Even if games were tough, you could bet your last sixpence that Kit would score. At times, he might look a little lazy but then he'd throw in a body swerve or a burst of pace and be away from whoever had been given the unenviable job of marking him.

I have never seen his like in an Albion shirt again and know I never will.

And back in 1967, for an 11-year-old boy, there was an added bonus of watching the Albion play - crisps and a drink at half-time and a bag of chips from a van outside the ground at the end of each game. So I was hooked for life and began a routine of a bus ride on the Number 26 from Mile Oak to the ground for a home match every fortnight, and a Football Combination (reserve game) on alternate Saturdays – the matches when you got to talk with the keeper during the game. And after a few months I was even allowed to go alone, or with a friend from school.

Then there came the waiting-in-line at the North-West corner gates for players' autographs after training sessions, during the school holidays, sugar paper scrapbooks of match cuttings from *The Argus* and the obligatory club scarf and a matching *Subbuteo* team. And, of course, learning the array of terrace chants of *"Cha Cha Cha Livesey… I'd go a million miles for one of your goals, oh Charleee,"* and the fact that every referee didn't have a father and was therefore a *"bastard"*. My favourite was a regular rendering of: *"Pull the chain, pull the chain, flush him away,"* usually directed at an opposition player.

This was what being a Brighton and Hove Albion fan was all about. It was an all-consuming schoolboy passion.

And a passion, which over 50 years has endured three divorces (at least one directly due to my love of football), living in Scotland, Yorkshire and the North East, the hellish fight for the survival of our club in the mid-1990s, the Gillingham and Withdean years and at last the glory of the Amex and our promotion to the promised land of the Premier League.

It remains a tight personal journey, a passion and a real story, which I hope the ensuing chapters will tell.

The years roll by and despite the changes, 25 managers and scores of players since 1967, the club remains Brighton and Hove Albion and we, the fans, remain its never changing life-blood.

In 1967, England were World Champions, Harold Wilson was Prime Minister, the newest must-have car was the Ford Escort, mods still fought rockers on Brighton beach, man had yet to land on the moon, colour TV was just a dream, Dick Knight was a mere 29 years old, Peter Ward was just 12, and Tony Bloom hadn't yet been born.

Yes, times really have changed…

My return bus journey to the Goldstone in 1967 was 4d (about 2p), admission to the North Stand was 2s 9d (13p) - a lot less for the reserve games - the match programme was 1s (5p), a cup of Bovril 2d (1p) and a bag of crisps the same.

So to travel and watch my heroes every Saturday, and enjoy a half-time snack cost a stately 21p!

To put things in perspective: in 1967 the average annual wage for a man was £900, the average mortgage was £90 a year and a loaf of bread was just 5p… a season ticket to watch the English champions Manchester United was £8.50. To allow for inflation, £1 in 1967 is worth £16.80 today (2019), so I'll let you the reader do the maths and comparisons.

In 2018, I returned to Mile Oak and the playground of my primary school years for the first time since we left the area in 1968. I was stunned by the changes that had occurred in the ensuing 50 years. The quiet roads and cul-de-sacs of new housing, where I had first kicked a football and played until the sun went down, were now a sea of parked cars and the bustling noise of revving engines.

And the open South Downs, where I used to roam, are now cut in two by the A27 Shoreham by-pass and tunnel. The former military training ground has disappeared, the old witch's cottage demolished, the isolation hospital flattened and childhood innocence all but vanquished. Only Mile Oak Farm – owned for generations by the Cross family - still remains.

Now, nearing retirement and sitting in front of a state-of-the-art PC with *Sergeant Pepper's Lonely Hearts Club Band* playing on the iPlayer, the years come tumbling back and memories of that blissful sunny Saturday in 1967 will never leave me.

I really did pop my cherry against Bury.

NOTE: A tragic irony is that when I wrote this first chapter in the late autumn of 2018, Kit Napier was still with us. On 1st April 2019, while I was making final revisions to the book, my hero Kit died, aged 75 at his adopted home in Durban, South Africa, after suffering from emphysema for many years. His 99 goal tally for the Albion was the most by any player in the post-war era, until overtaken in the 2018/19 season by Glenn Murray.

I am sure Kit has gone to join Charlie Livesey, Nobby Lawton, Wally Gould and others in an Albion *Field of Dreams* somewhere.

The Albion finished the 1967/68 season 10th in League Division Three with 48 points. Champions were Oxford United on 57 points and runners-up were Bury.

Top scorer was my hero Kit Napier with a stunning 28 goals. Kit was to be the club's top scorer for five out of six seasons between 1967 and 1972. No Brighton player would score more than 28 goals in a season until the arrival of Peter Ward in 1976.

Please note that until 1992, the English football leagues were named: League Division One, League Division Two, League Division Three and League Division Four. With the creation of the Premier League in 1993, the other divisions were subtly renamed League Division 1, League Division 2 and League Division 3. Things changed again in 2005 with the creation of the Championship, and the lower two divisions were renamed League One and League Two.

Who Ate All the Pies? Bury

I have only watched Brighton play Bury half a dozen times over the past 50 years. But, four of those occasions have been at Bury's homely Gigg Lane, just north of Manchester. There is only one food associated with games against the Shakers: a Black Pudding muffin (the local name for a bread bun) or better still a Black Pudding and Bacon muffin. If fried pig's blood is not your taste, then a Chip Muffin with plenty of brown sauce will have to do!

Chapter Two

Snowballs and a Very Rude Sausage
Vicarage Road
28 December 1968

Watford's Vicarage Road ground circa 1970

During the spring of 1968, due to my father's job change, our family moved house to the village of Apsley, near Hemel Hempstead, in far flung Hertfordshire.

It was only 86 miles from Mile Oak, but for a 12-year-old boy without any access to a telephone, and long before the internet, it might as well have been Venus.

Suddenly my whole life was turned upside down. Not only was I losing many friends, whom I had known for all my early years, but I was also being denied my regular visits to the Goldstone Ground and my Brighton and Hove Albion.

Our new home was a spacious Victorian coaching house nestling on the busy Belswains Lane, which years later would lead directly to the M25 motorway.

My ground floor bedroom of this old building, quickly decorated with dozens of pictures of my Albion heroes - cut from copies of the Argus, home football programmes and *Goal* magazine - was my only sanctuary.

And the slow search for new friends began.

I quickly discovered that any new school associate scoffed when I mentioned Brighton and Hove Albion… *"Who are they?"* they would answer with friendly scorn. This was an area where everyone supported Watford and hated Luton Town. And if you weren't on this particular football bus then you were an outsider.

So denied of my beloved Albion, I acquiesced and soon began accompanying these new friends to watch Watford… spending each game nestled at the front of the Rookery End (the home terraced stand) at Vicarage Road.

As the 1968/69 season kicked off, I began a routine of attending every Watford home game – and it was going to be some ride as this was the season they drew with European Champions Manchester United in the FA Cup and then pipped both Swindon and Luton Town to the League Division Three title winning promotion to League Division Two (the Championship).

Their 1-0 home win against Plymouth Argyle, which sealed promotion, was my first pitch invasion and a taste of proper football success – albeit with an adopted club!

And sandwiched in the middle of this season was a home game against Brighton and Hove Albion.

Meanwhile, I kept in touch by snail post with two Albion-obsessed friends from back home in Hove. Letter writing became a new pursuit as Rob and Andy began sending me match day programmes and back page cuttings from the *Argus*, in exchange for Watford goodies – quite why either of them wanted anything related to Watford is still beyond me!

For the next four years this remained my only regular way of keeping in touch with the Albion, bar an odd family trip back to Sussex to stay with my maternal grandparents in Shoreham by Sea. But then came the big day and the best Christmas present I could have wished for!

It was a particularly cold winter in 1968. Over the festive period there was an unforecast White Christmas, with heavy snow falling across a large part of the country overnight on Christmas Eve and into Christmas morning. A depth of four inches was recorded in parts of Hertfordshire with some rural areas seeing up to 10 inches of snow falling on Christmas Day.

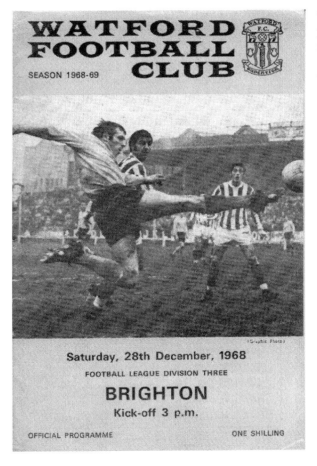

The match day programme featuring Watford's striker Barry Endean on the cover

For a 12-year-old boy it was a white heaven, but at that time I was naively unaware of the havoc the freezing weather would have on football – long before the years of undersoil heated pitches.

Beyond Christmas, the weather remained cold and wintry up until the New Year, with snow cover lasting.

But nothing would stop me attending Vicarage Road on Saturday 28th December to watch Watford entertain Brighton and Hove Albion.

So wrapped up in my dark green Parka with gloves and a neutral coloured scarf I met my school mates, Alex, John and Matt, at our usual spot at the front of the Rookery End. I promised not to cheer for Brighton as long as they promised not to "dob" me in to the older Watford supporters.

To be frank, even as a young Albion fanatic, I wasn't expecting much from this game. Watford had the meanest defence in all of the Football League – at the end of the season their 25 clean sheets remained a League record for the next 50 years.

Plus they had already beaten us 1-0 in the first fixture at the Goldstone Ground in October.

The only unknown since Christmas Day was whether the snow and ice might lead to the game being postponed or even abandoned.

But on Friday, in sub-zero temperatures, the canny Vicarage Road ground staff – with help from dozens of local people – covered the entire pitch with straw in an effort to keep the surface playable. And it worked!

The game at Vicarage Road was one of only a few to go ahead in the London area on that cold winter weekend.

The same ground staff spent Saturday morning clearing the straw to the red gravel greyhound track which ran around the outside of the pitch.

Bizarrely this mound of straw held a strange fascination for four pre-teen boys during a largely uneventful first half in front of 12,536 fans.

"Look, they've buried one of the ball boys!" yelled John, pointing to a hump in the straw.

"He must be fuckin' cold!" laughed Alex, *"Look at his willy!"* sticking his gloved finger towards a rather large hot dog sausage which was poking through the straw.

"Isn't it red!" added Matt, *"he must be freezing!"*

16

Suddenly four pairs of eyes were glued towards the sausage. We were all laughing out loud.

There followed more schoolboy sniggers and rude jokes as the sausage became the focus of our attention until half time.

"I bet Stewart Scullion's sausage is bigger than that!" shouted one girl wearing a Watford scarf.

Either side might have scored a goal, but not one of us would have seen it, such was the pre-pubescent fascination with this rude looking hot dog sausage.

Snowball man, the Albion skipper and central defender John Napier © The Argus

On the pitch, Kit Napier showed flashes of brilliance and came close to scoring twice, while Nobby Lawton and Bobby Smith battled in midfield. But there was none of the attacking flare I had been used to seeing at the Goldstone Ground before our move to Hertfordshire. This was my first taste of how we played away from home.

Meanwhile, as the whistle blew for half-time, we had been joined at the front of the Rookery by half a dozen other boys in our now public and ongoing sausage joke.

It was 0-0 as the players slowly trooped off towards the changing rooms, through a tunnel in the centre of the old grandstand.

But then our attention was unexpectedly distracted from the sausage.

The Brighton players were getting the usual verbal abuse from a section of the home fans standing at the left end of the grandstand, when someone in the crowd threw a snowball at a random player.

There were loud shouts of glee from other Watford fans as another snowball was thrown, which hit our centre back John Napier on the shoulder, splattering ice cold snow across his right neck and cheek.

Quick as a flash, the 6ft 2in Irishman bent down, shouted something towards the crowd and made a large snowball himself before hurling it back in the direction of the Watford supporters.

From where we were standing in the adjoining Rookery End none of us could see whether the snowball hit anyone, but we could hear the reaction from the Watford fans near to the incident, who were hurling even more abuse towards our skipper.

But the referee did see the snowball being thrown.

So as the players continued towards the dressing room, our centre back was booked (these are the days before yellow cards) for "ungentlemanly conduct" and given a serious talking to by the ref.

Following the game, John Napier had no comment to make when questioned about the incident.

One thing is certain… if any player did something similar today, he would be sent off, fined by his club and the FA, and probably banned for a half a dozen games.

But these were very different times.

To show how much times have changed in English league football: less than three years later at Vicarage Road, Watford centre forward Barry Endean was similarly only booked after taking down his shorts and baring his naked buttocks to Oxford United fans in a 4th Round FA Cup replay.

Endean was far from coy or apologetic about his misdemeanour. After the game he told the press: *"There were only a couple of minutes left.*

The crowd was irritating me. I pulled down my shorts. I mean ... we were almost out of the Cup. I was near to tears," was his reasoning.

These were certainly were different times.

Watford beat Brighton and Hove Albion 1-0 with a late header from their regular impact substitute Rodney Green, for whom the Watford fans coined the chant: *"Rodney Green, Rodney Green, He's the biggest substitute you've ever seen."*

On the train home, Matt, John and Alex were too busy laughing about the sausage and the snowballs, to give me much grief about the scoreline.

Watford went on to win League Division Three in the 1968/69 season with 64 points, with Swindon Town as runners-up. Brighton and Hove Albion finished 12th on 45 points. Top scorer was once again Kit Napier, this time with 18 goals.

Who Ate All the Pies? Watford

Pie and Mash is traditionally a Watford favourite. But for the sake of this chapter the chosen food has to be a large hot dog with fried onions and ketchup – still the fans' choice at most football grounds in the country. Some posh clubs even offer it in French bread!

Chapter Three

Ley off Kit's shirt!
The Goldstone Ground
13 August 1969

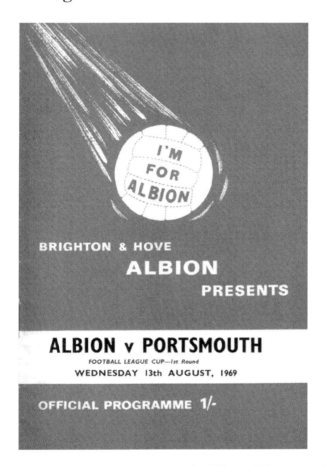

BRIGHTON & HOVE
ALBION
PRESENTS

ALBION v PORTSMOUTH
FOOTBALL LEAGUE CUP—1st Round
WEDNESDAY 13th AUGUST, 1969

OFFICIAL PROGRAMME **1/-**

And so it comes to pass, the **Rite of Passage** for any young football fan... the first night game without an adult chaperone. My own Rite of Passage happened unexpectedly and was unique to me for at least three reasons:

1. I happened by sheer chance to be back in East Sussex on holiday
2. It was still summer and the evening sky was still blue
3. It remains one of the greatest Albion matches I have ever seen

As I already mentioned, I had managed to keep in touch with two school friends from Hove since our family moved to Hertfordshire in the spring of 1968.

Rob and Andy had kept me alive with regular parcels of match day programmes, but other than the away game at Watford, my last Brighton game at the Goldstone was to watch a 1-0 victory against Southport on 30th March 1968.

Then, with the 1969 school summer holidays in full swing, I had arranged with my parents to stay with Rob in Portslade for a week. In return, he would stay for a further week with me at my new home in Apsley.

My dad had driven me the 80 odd miles to Rob's house in Portslade on Saturday 9th August and over the next few days we played, went to Southwick summer fair, and mucked around as most 13-year-old boys do.

It was a refreshing change and I guess I was beginning to experience some real independence for the first time in my life – probably partly due to my mum being preoccupied with my new baby sister.

Within hours of arriving, Rob told me he had already arranged for us both to see Brighton play the "mighty" Portsmouth in a First Round League Cup tie on the Wednesday evening (13th August). Pompey were a high flying and established League Division Two (Championship) club, while we were still a mediocre third tier side by comparison, albeit under a young and progressive manager, Freddie Goodwin.

We both believed that a draw to take Portsmouth back to Fratton Park for a replay would be a good result… probably the best we could hope for.

As things turned out, that was not to be.

After a tea of egg and chips, Rob and I boarded a bus for the short journey along the Old Shoreham Road to our beloved Mecca of the Goldstone Ground.

With the sun shining on a warm August evening, we entered the 'juvenile' gates at the west side of the North Stand. Rob quickly led me to the spot where he bravely claimed he stood for every home game… two thirds the way back in the centre of the stand behind the goal.

Ensconced with a match day programme and a bag of crisps, I began to soak in the atmosphere as the ground filled up.

Around us were towering adults, including one 20-something guy to my left who was wearing a Chelsea shirt and who seemed to spend the entire game talking to his mate about a forthcoming game with West Ham!

The air was thick with cigarette smoke and a steam of body odour mixed with testosterone and Bovril.

Voices chattered everywhere, broken only by guffaws of adult laughter, obscenities and the occasional yell. As kick-off approached, the Albion chants began around us: *"It's Brighton Hove Albion, Brighton Hove Albion FC, we're by far the greatest team, the world has ever seen"*, followed by a quick *"Zigger Zagger, Zigger, Zagger, oi oi oi."*

We quickly became aware that a noisy Portsmouth section was well over to our left towards the east terracing as their own chants echoed back… with niceties like: *"You're gonna get your fucking heads kicked in,"* and the even more pointed: *"You're going home in an ambulance."*

The summer evening air and local rivalry had brought out an atmosphere and a menace to the terraces I had previously yet to witness.

The chanting and singing were never-ending and I tried to join in where I could. By kick-off, the North Stand was ram jammed full – the attendance that night was 19,787 – and it was the largest football crowd I had ever witnessed.

Bodies massed and bodies swayed as the game got underway.

It was claustrophobic but exhilarating at the same time.

I jockeyed forward a bit for a better sight of the pitch.

We were attacking the North Stand.

And our heroes in their blue shirts with white sleeves were more than holding their own.

WATNEYS ALES

SOLD IN ALL
BARS HERE

ALBION		PORTSMOUTH	
(Blue Shirts, White Shorts)		(Red Shirts and Shorts)	
1	Geoff SIDEBOTTOM	1	John MILKINS
2	Stewart HENDERSON	2	Mike TRAVERS
3	Willie BELL	3	George LEY
4	Bobby SMITH	4	David MUNKS
5	John NAPIER	5	Eoin HAND
6	Dave TURNER	6	Tom YOULDEN
7	Kit NAPIER	7	Albert McCANN
8	Nobby LAWTON	8	Ray POINTER
9	Alex DAWSON	9	Bill ATKINS
10	Alan GILLIVER	10	Brian BROMLEY
11	Eddie SPEARRITT	11	Ray HIRON
12	David ARMSTRONG	12	Harry HARRIS

Referee: B. H. DANIELS, Rainham

Linesmen: K. BRAY, Uxbridge (Red Flag)

R. E. EVANS, Upminster (Yellow Flag)

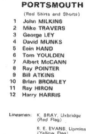

NEXT MATCHES AT THE GOLDSTONE

● Saturday, August 23rd — K.O. 3 p.m.
ALBION versus BOURNEMOUTH

● WEDNESDAY, AUG. 27—K.O. 7.30 p.m.
ALBION versus ROCHDALE

Nobby Lawton was commanding midfield and every pass seemed to find someone in blue. In attack, Bobby Smith, Alan Gilliver and Eddie Spearritt again and again took the ball to the Pompey defence.

But then the game suddenly exploded into life.

After a succession of Albion corners, a cross was whipped into the crowded Portsmouth box from the left, and boom! With the ball seeming to hang under the lights, big Alex Dawson – who looked like a scarred nightclub bouncer - leapt above his marker and powered a header destined for the back of the net.

But it cruelly rebounded off the crossbar and was eventually scrambled clear.

A few minutes later another Dawson header, this time assisted by a dink into the box by Lawton, was saved by Pompey keeper John Milkins. We were on top and it was surely only a matter of time before we would score.

The roars from around the ground were loud as the half-time whistle blew.

24

Back in the North Stand, the minute break was punctuated by more aggressive chanting from both sets of fans – separated only by a flimsy fence and a few police officers. *"You're gonna get your fucking heads kicked in,"* was returned with: *"You're going home like Sandy Richardson"* – a cruel reference to a wheelchair bound actor in the TV soap **Crossroads**.

Then word spread that a hundred Portsmouth fans had broken through and were trying to run the North Stand from the east terracing. Within minutes, the word became a reality. Coins, cans and lit cigarettes were being thrown in the dimly lit dusk of the stand; fans started to surge in different directions and a sense of panic circulated before the police moved in and made arrests and ejections amid both sets of supporters.

So was this the football violence I had heard so much about on TV? It was tribal and oddly fascinating, frightening and exhilarating all at the same time.

The rumbles continued, but thankfully, other than more rabid chanting, the simmering tension and sporadic fighting was kept under control.

And now more importantly, as the second half kicked off under brilliant floodlights, the Albion were on the attack again.

Within minutes we almost scored but Pompey defender George Ley powered a goal-bound Alan Gilliver header off the line.

It was now all Brighton as our midfield made more penetrating inroads into the Portsmouth defence.

An autumn mist from the sweating bodies was beginning to swirl in the air under the floodlights as the chanting became louder.

Then with just 10 minutes of the second half played it happened! Full back Willie Bell found Dawson on the edge of the box and his shot had too much power for Milkins, who got a hand to it but could only watch as it soared into the top of the net.

The North and South stands rocked and rolled while the whole ground erupted in a cacophony of noise. At that time in my young life I had never experienced an atmosphere like it.

The Albion players rejoiced in front of our delirious fans, while two Portsmouth defenders fell to their knees with their keeper Milkins remonstrating loudly.

We were winning!

Dawson was razor sharp and a few minutes later when Lawton hit a long ball into the goal-mouth, he was there again. A little high with his effort, but he was running riot amidst the Pompey defence.

As time began to run out for the visitors, there were two flare-ups. With less than 15 minutes to go and Pompey pressing, Kit Napier received the ball near the centre circle and broke forward at pace. He had split the Portsmouth defence and was racing into their half and towards the South Stand goal with the ball at his feet.

The Brighton and Hove Albion squad 1969/70   © **The Argus**

His marker, George Ley, was beaten for both pace and by Kit's skill, when the unthinkable happened... Ley reached out and grabbed Napier's number 7 shirt. The North Stand screamed *"Foul"* in one voice as the shirt was quite literally ripped off his back. With the Albion fans still seething and Napier's shirt flapping behind him, referee Brian Daniels blew for a foul. Surprisingly, Ley, who later played for the Albion, did not even get booked. But at least we had a free kick and another chance to attack the Portsmouth goal... a gliding header from Alex Dawson narrowly missing to the right. Then two minutes from the end of the game Pompey's Tom Youlden was booked for deliberately kicking Alan Gilliver. The final 10 minutes were tense, but the Albion held on for a famous victory under the lights.

An FA Cup 4th Round tie against Chelsea in February 1967 and Kit gets the better of Ron "Chopper" Harris. Throughout his years at the Albion, Kit's turn of speed could get him past most defenders © The Argus

I had lost Rob in the celebrations, but caught up with him later on the bus journey back to his house. I had a feeling from his sheepish smile that he had been ejected from the North Stand during the rumpus at half-time, as he had no obvious memory of the second half of the game. I kept shtum as it was clear he did not want his parents to know of his misdemeanour.

As for me, I had passed through my own Rite of Passage as a Brighton and Hove Albion supporter and 50 years later the events and atmosphere of that amazing evening remain with me as if it were yesterday.

The 1969/70 season was a good one for the Albion. In the second round of the League Cup we beat League Division Two Birmingham City 2-0, before narrowly succumbing 2-3 to First Division Wolverhampton Wanderers in the Third Round. We finished the season in fifth place in League Division Three, just five points shy of promotion. The Albion had to wait two more years for promotion into League Division Two.

27

Who Ate All the Pies? Portsmouth

At every football ground in England, Scotland and Wales I have attended (there are more than 80) the go-to half time drink is always hot Bovril.

And synonymous with seaside grounds such as the Goldstone and Portsmouth's Fratton Park are Crab Sticks – or Seafood Sticks as they are now called, after someone pointed out that they don't contain any crab meat!

Chapter Four

Is This a Record? No, it's a Damned Disgrace!
The Goldstone Ground
1 December 1973

Brian Clough with Mike Bamber at Brighton yesterday.

The Daily Mirror, 2 November 1973   © The Daily Mirror

So after four years exile in Hertfordshire my family returned to live in Sussex during the summer of 1972.

Once again the move was due to my father's work, and it was just in time for me to start studying for my A Levels in the local sixth form.

But it was a time of celebration for me, as I could once again reignite a more tangible love affair with Brighton and Hove Albion and my beloved Goldstone Ground.

This time our new home was in North Lancing… a little further from Hove, and close to where the Albion's Elite Football Performance Centre now stands.

The summer move gave me time to bed-in watching - or rather crying about – my heroes for a whole season.

The one thing about following Brighton and Hove Albion is that we rarely do mid-table mediocrity - it is either high rise elation or total despair. And our 1972/73 season in League Division Two remains one of the worst I have seen Albion play.

We managed only eight victories all season. We were poor at home and lambs to the slaughter away… a 6-2 drubbing at Blackpool, 5-1 at Carlisle, 4-0 at Sunderland and 5-1 at Fulham were just a small taste of how poor we really were.

We finished the season bottom of the table on 29 points, with 83 goals conceded and were relegated back to League Division Three. Most fans believed it would spell the end of Pat Saward's three-year tenure as Brighton and Hove Albion manager.

But, club chairman Mike Bamber remained loyal to the man who had guided the Albion to promotion just 15 months earlier. This loyalty was however stretched to breaking point as we began our 1973/74 season back in the third tier in a similar appalling fashion. And the writing was on the wall for dear Pat.

His departure was clarified after we suffered six successive home defeats at the start of the campaign, and another relegation seemed to be on the horizon.

Pat Saward was eventually sacked on 23rd October 1973.

His dismissal was confirmed publicly in the press and on TV by no-nonsense Mike Bamber.

"Pat Saward has been sacked. The decision was made after the game with Shrewsbury (a scrappy 2-0 victory) *on Saturday evening. The parting has been on the cards for some weeks,"* said the chairman.

"We have had six home defeats and are down to crowds of 5,000 wonderful people. No club can live on such gates."

But Mr Bamber's next comment was to prove telling: *"We will come to an agreement with Mr Saward over his contract. We have not approached anybody and will be advertising the job and hope to get a really top manager."*

Meanwhile, Glen Wilson, the trainer, was made responsible for running the playing side of the club, assisted by youth team coach Ray Crawford. Their tenure lasted just two games.

The Brighton and Hove Albion squad 1973/74   © **The Argus**

The managerial machinations of a run-of-the-mill League Division Three football club like Brighton and Hove Albion were low key. But, 190 miles away the whole of English football had been rocked by the news that Derby County's brilliant management duo of Brian Clough and Peter Taylor had resigned.

Clough and Taylor had transformed Derby from a club pottering about in the League Division Two to champions of England and European Cup semi-finalists. He was the people's choice as next England manager and yet his next stop was to be manager of Brighton and Hove Albion.

Following six days of negotiations with Mike Bamber, the astonishing coup was pulled off in a Derby hotel on the evening of Wednesday 31st October and announced to the world the next morning.

Just seven days after Pat Saward's dismissal!

Brian Clough's first match in charge of the Albion was a drab 0-0 draw against York City at the Goldstone, on 3rd November.

There followed two more dreary draws against Huddersfield Town and Chesterfield and a narrow 1-0 win against Walsall, followed by a mortifying 4-0 home defeat to non-league Walton and Hersham in a FA Cup 1st round replay, after being held to a 0-0 draw at their place the previous weekend.

Whatever was wrong with Albion's form over the previous 15 months, it was going to take a miracle from Brian Clough to fix it. That miracle gained astronomical proportions three days later with the visit to the Goldstone by division pace-setters Bristol Rovers and their rampant *Smash and Grab* nicknamed strike partnership of Bruce Bannister and Alan Warboys.

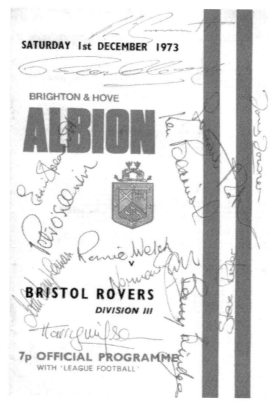

A signed match programme from that dismal day at the Goldstone Ground in December 1973

Clough's new charges were about to become a frozen sacrifice to humiliation on a cold winter's day. It is a game which also remains frozen in my memory for all the wrong reasons.

Early that morning after wrapping up in a warm winter coat with my Albion scarf around my neck, I hopped on the train from Lancing Station for the 15-minute journey to Hove.

On the walk to the Goldstone, I met sixth form friends Tony and John and we ambled together up to the Old Shoreham Road.

We had all witnessed the previous months of Albion's dismal run of form and despite all the hurrah and expectation attached to Clough's arrival, we were not expecting much from this game.

After buying a bag of chips and a hotdog each from a van outside the ground, we made our way into the North Stand and stood near the upper middle behind the goal.

The crowd was 10,762, a lot larger than most of our home games for the previous 10 months, but still the ground only felt half-full and the Bristol Rovers fans were making a lot of noise.

We kept ourselves warm by jumping up and down and clapping our hands. We viewed the frozen mud in the near goal mouth with some trepidation... we all still had frosted memories of the FA Cup defeat three days earlier and it was clear that pitch had not recovered. But that was not going to excuse what was about to happen.

In the North Stand, only the presence of Brian Clough as manager kept up any enthusiasm in a game we felt sure we would lose. Quite the magnitude of that loss we had yet to witness.

However, with a team which included the experience of Brian Powney in goal, the ever-dependable Norman Gall, Peter O'Sullivan, George Ley, Eddie Spearritt and Tony Towner we felt we would at least make a game of it.

How wrong we all were!

For what happened at the Goldstone that day was the worst home defeat in the English Football League since Wolves beat Cardiff 9-1 at Ninian Park in a League Division One match in 1955-56.

Without dwelling or making any excuses, it is better just to recount the goals, which rolled into Powney's net like buses on the Old Shoreham Road.

5 minutes: Former Albion player Colin Dobson set it up. Warboys streaked down the left wing, beat Norman Gall near the by-line, and Bannister timed his run to fire the first goal. (0-1) *Ouch!*

12 minutes: Dobson took Warboys' pass, and laid on a pinpointed centre for Fearnley's header. (0-2) *Bugger!*

20 minutes: A deceptive shot by Peter O'Sullivan swerved and kept low gave the Albion a glimmer of hope. (1-2) *We have hope.*

29 minutes: An overlap by Jacobs spelled danger when Ley missed his tackle and from the cross Bannister's head did the rest. (1-3) *Hope evaporating.*

32 minutes: Powney failed to hold a hard, low free kick from Warboys, and Bannister tapped the rebound into the net. (1-4) *Oh Powney, you goon!*

39 minutes: Another Dobson centre, and Warboys started his own personal rampage. (1-5) *Is there a word stronger than "fuck"?*

55 minutes: Bannister turned goal maker by laying this one on for Warboys. (1-6) *This is truly embarrassing.*

63 minutes: Warboys raced through on a pass from Parson. Out came Powney, but he had no chance. (1-7) *At least Powney tried but fans are starting to leave the ground already.*

70 minutes: Albion appealed for offside against Warboys, but he went on to score easily. (1-8) *Rovers could make double figures.*

87 minutes: A floating Tony Towner centre, and Ronnie Howell banged in a well-taken consolation goal. (2-8) *We really scored!*

Smash and Grab: **Bristol Rovers' deadly duo of Bruce Bannister and Alan Warboys**

The humiliation was complete as the die-hard North Stand sheepishly cheered the final goal. It was truly a relief when the ref blew his whistle for the end of the game. The silence after that was palpable. There were even a few ironic chants of *"Clough Out!"* But we all realised that it was not the new manager's fault, but the group of players he had inherited, the loss of team confidence and a freefall of form over the past 15 months.

After conceding 12 goals in just four days we all needed to get home to the warmth of our families and try to forget what we had witnessed.

"Is that a record?" I asked my two mates as we walked to the train station.

"No," quipped Tony, *"It's a bloody disgrace."*

Although I was to witness many more humiliating defeats with the Albion, this was the biggest and the most memorable.

A month into the job and Clough was left under no illusions about the size of the reconstruction his new team required.

The day after the cataclysmic loss he didn't flinch when it came to his on-screen duties for *ITV's* **The Big Match** - the TV cameras had been in attendance at the Goldstone Ground. Clough sat in the London TV studio and forensically dissected the way the Albion defence had conceded each and every one of the eight goals Bristol Rovers had put past them.

A week later the Albion were thrashed 4-1 at Tranmere before succumbing to single goal defeats against Watford and Aldershot. We slipped to 20th position in League Division Three, one place above the drop zone.

As for Bristol Rovers, their amazing form continued. Unsurprisingly, they were promoted with a game to spare. They finished the season with the return fixture against the Albion at the Eastville Stadium. Rovers' fans expected they would again maul the softies from the south coast, but it never materialised. Albion's Lamie Robertson opened the scoring after a neat one-two with Ken Beamish on 19 minutes. It took Bruce Bannister's late penalty to level the score.

Whatever anyone's views about his time as manager of Brighton and Hove Albion and Leeds United, Brian Clough remains a true legend of the English game, with statues to him in Middlesbrough, Derby and Nottingham

Brian Clough was in charge at Brighton and Hove Albion for 35 games from the beginning of November 1973 to the end of April 1974. His tenure was brief, but he changed the way Albion played and he laid a firm foundation for his associate Peter Taylor to develop, which would lead to the signing of Peter Ward and eventually promotion back to League Division Two and the hacienda Alan Mullery years of the late 1970s.

Brighton and Hove Albion finished the 1973/74 League Division Three season in 19th place with 43 points. The champions were Oldham Athletic on 62 points and runners-up were Bristol Rovers on 61 points. Alan Warboys scored 53 league goals for Bristol Rovers between 1972 and 1976, while his strike partner bagged 80 league goals in 206 appearances over the same period. But *Smash and Grab* never again emulated the 40 goals they scored in the 1973/74 season as part of Rovers 32-game unbeaten run.

Who Ate All the Pies? Bristol

Whether watching the Albion play Bristol Rovers at their old Eastville Stadium or at the newer Memorial Stadium, or even Bristol City at Ashton Gate, you're spoilt for amazing food. Due to the city's huge West Indian heritage, there is a wide and wonderful choice of Caribbean street food from vendors parked near the grounds. So Jamaican Jerk Chicken with rice and peas in a paper bowl with a wooden spoon either before or after a game is a must!

Chapter Five

A Sublime Day in May
St James Park
5 May 1979

Four of Newcastle's famous seven bridges over the Tyne

My paternal grandfather's abiding passions were his vegetable garden, barley wine, horse racing and Newcastle United Football Club – not necessarily in that order.

But one thing was certain, enter his living room any time after 4.40 on a Saturday afternoon - once the BBC tele-printer was running - and there was complete silence, as he waited for the Newcastle result to come in.

Grandfather, or Pop as he was known, was born and raised in Throckley, seven miles west of Newcastle upon Tyne, the son and grandson of coal miners at the village's Maria Pit. He was a Geordie to the bones.

He had moved south in 1933, during the Depression, with my gran, my dad and his three siblings, to find better work and a better life.

Then following the death of my grandmother in 1978, and coupled with his own failing health, aged 86, he returned north early in the early spring of 1979. He wanted to live out his final years on his beloved Tyneside in the picturesque small village of Corbridge.

All my young life he had regaled me with a deep passion for the pre-war Newcastle teams (particularly the 1926/27 League Division One champions) and for the three-times post war FA Cup winners, with the legendary centre forward Jackie Milburn – the uncle of Bobby and Jack Charlton.

So we come to the evening of Friday 4th May, 1979, and I am sipping a large whisky with Pop at his comfortable new home in Corbridge and talking excitedly about the reason I am staying with him for the weekend. I am enthusing about my beloved Brighton and Hove Albion and their end of season fixture at St James Park against his equally beloved Magpies.

He smiles, asks me to pour him another whisky – this time with a splash of ginger wine - and whispers: *"Don't get carried away, lad, your team haven't done it yet, they still have to encounter the Mags on God's own soil."*

We continued talking – or rather me listening – about football and sport in general till late in the evening.

I went to bed that night with a huge grin on my face.

Saturday 5th May was our big day and I barely slept that night in anticipation of the big match.

But strangely, our promotion deciding match in May wasn't the last day of the 1978/79 season.

A snow-laden winter had left many clubs playing catch-up with their remaining fixtures, and we were going into our last game at Newcastle, at the top of a remarkably tight League Division Two table, with just one point separating the top four clubs.

A win would secure us promotion to League Division One for the first time in our history, against a Newcastle side in ninth place, with little to play for, bar pride.

So that morning, in bright sunshine, but with a chill wind in the air, I hopped on the local train into the city.

At Newcastle station I met an old friend named Pete – a Geordie with whom I had gone to many Newcastle games while we were at university together in West Yorkshire. He had a black and white scarf wrapped around his neck and was grinning widely.

"Why aye, Nic, let's do some beer," he enthused, *"There are a few pubs that open at 10.30."*

And so we began a two-man pub crawl for the short distance between the city station and the Newcastle ground.

After a lunch of Stottie, Pease Pudding and gravy in the Grainger Market, we eventually reached The Strawberry, an infamous drinking hole outside the Gallowgate End of St James Park. It was (and still is) a pub for home supporters only.

"Keep yer trap shut inside," Pete winked, *"Or I am not responsible for taking you to hospital! And don't forget you drink the broon in a half pint glass, so don't complain,"* he added, smiling broadly.

The Gallowgate End or "Gallows Hole" was an historic place of public execution in Newcastle. In 1650, 22 people - including 15 witches - were hanged in one day.

The last hanging took place in 1844, only three decades before the first ball was kicked inside St James Park!

So I drank my pint of Newcastle Brown in the regulation half pint glass quietly, to avoid becoming a 20th century execution!

The Brighton and Hove Albion squad in the 1978/79 season © The Argus

Then, merry with beer, Pete and I shook hands and wended our respective ways to either end of this legendary football stadium. What followed was the stuff of real legends.

The weather was sunny and slightly windy as the game kicked off with more than 10,000 Albion fans cheering our team on as part of a St James' Park crowd of 28,434.

But as the match progressed it rained, it snowed and it hailed… after all this was the North East!

Our team that day was full of many players who would become club legends. With Eric Steele in goal behind a defence of Chris Cattlin, Gary Williams, Andy Rollings and Paul Clark there was a buzzing midfield of skipper Brian Horton, Gerry Ryan, Peter Sayer and Peter O'Sullivan and a strike partnership of Peter Ward and Teddy Maybank.

Skipper Brian Horton turns away after scoring Albion's first goal

The first 10 minutes were all Albion as we attacked the Leazes End, where our supporters were gathered. We were dominating, then suddenly from a left wing Gary Williams' corner, Brian Horton snuck between the square Newcastle defence to bullet a header into the net. (1-0 Albion).

With Rollings and Cattlin immense in our own defence, Horton running the midfield, and Peter Ward inspiring, Albion began

41

bossing the game. A few minutes later, Ward let Maybank in with a clear shot on goal, but Teddy shanked the ball wide.

That was the key for Newcastle to up their game, and they twice came close to an equaliser.

But they hadn't counted on Peter Ward, who made a ghosting run through their defence – reminiscent of Kit Napier - before carefully directing a shot, which somehow managed to cross the goal line (2-0 Albion).

Our football was expansive as the rain started to teem down and passes from both sides went astray as the grass became increasingly slippery.

It was end to end stuff, before Ward fired at goal and Gerry Ryan poked in the rebound from a Newcastle defender. (3-0 Albion).

It was scarcely believable. Here we were top of the table and leading the mighty Newcastle United 3-0 and playing some amazing football. All around me the chanting didn't cease, interspersed with laughter and whoops of joy. The sense of excitement was oozing from everyone. We were on the verge of the greatest moment in our club's history.

But the Magpies were not about to give up and with their own supporters yelling, they began to put steady pressure on our goal before the half-time whistle blew.

We were almost there… just 45 minutes to make history.

The second half was rocky in comparison as Brighton nerves coruscated their way around St James Park. But the clock was ticking and when Alan Shoulder pulled one back for Newcastle, it was too late for a comeback.

As the final whistle blew, the moment (and the game) was savoured. We went wild as our heroes in yellow ran towards us, manager Alan Mullery also raced onto the pitch, hugged his skipper Brian Horton and joined in the celebrations right in front of us.

Press and TV camera men were everywhere capturing the moment for posterity.

We strained our necks to get a better view. Tears flowed, voices shouted, cheers echoed, hugs were exchanged with total strangers and smiles enveloped every face.

The famous Strawberry pub at the Gallowgate End of St James Park as it was in the 1970s

We were promoted to the top flight for the first time in our history! Many years later Peter Ward still has very strong memories of that day.

"It was one of the most nerve-wracking games I ever experienced," he said.

"Looking back now, having won 3-1, it seems like it was quite a straight-forward result, but it was actually not like that at the time.

"The pressure on us was huge – we were 90 minutes away from the club winning promotion to the top division for the first time in their history, having missed out by a hair's breadth the previous season.

"But despite that pressure, we went out there and were unbelievable.

"Newcastle did pull one back in the second half, but as we got towards the final whistle, we were able to enjoy the last few moments of the game as we knew we were going up.

"It was a fantastic feeling when that final whistle blew and then the trip home from Newcastle - by a special train –the Pullman Brighton Belle - was one big party.

"Incredibly when we arrived back into Brighton station, at about 1 o'clock in the morning, there were thousands more supporters, who had not been able to travel up to Newcastle for the game, waiting for us to keep the party going!"

My own celebrations that day were much more muted, but equally special to me.

I have no idea what time I eventually left the ground. After the game I tried to find Pete for a celebratory pint, but in the days before mobile phones, and amid thousands of cheering supporters, the task was impossible. So I bought myself a pint of Newcastle Brown in a small pub near the station and hopped on the train back to Corbridge at about 7pm.

A few days later, Pete telephoned me at my home in Barnsley to say: *"Where were you afterwards? We were all waiting for you in The Strawberry!"*

I laughed and answered: *"Yeah, right!"*

But later that sublime Saturday evening I arrived back at Pop's home, to be greeted with a smile, a handshake, a *"well done, lad"* and a very large whisky.

"There's a few bottles of Broon in the kitchen if you'd rather," he smiled.

We sat together in his warm sitting room and for a change I regaled him about my beloved Brighton and Hove Albion.

Pop sadly passed away, two years later.

I will never forget him, nor that sublime day in May.

Brighton and Hove Albion's promotion to League Division One really had gone down to the wire. With a game in hand, Crystal Palace won the League Division Two title with 57 points, we were second on 56, just ahead of Stoke on goal difference and Sunderland fourth on 55 points.

Newcastle United finished 8th on 40 points.

Who Ate All the Pies? Newcastle

Essential pre- or post-match fayre in Newcastle upon Tyne (and Sunderland) is a Stottie (doughy white bread bap) and Pease Pudding or Pease Pudding and ham. Also popular is Stottie and gravy, Stottie and chips or Stottie and curry sauce. Washed down with a bottle of Newcastle Brown, or *Broon* as it is commonly called.

Chapter Six

Ernie Wise Frozen in Leeds
Elland Road
29 November 1980

Eric Morecambe and Leeds' very own Little Ern

All my adult life I have had an almost irrational tribal hatred for Leeds United… but more than that, I hate Elland Road with a vengeance.
The irrationality of my hatred of Leeds United is quite perverse as I have a very fond affinity for the city itself.

The hatred is also quite strange, because, as a young teenager, growing up in the outer reaches of Hove, they were always my so-called "big club" - the sort of club that most kids are drawn to when their own home town team is struggling in the lower reaches of the football league. A passing phase that most of us grow out of sooner rather than later.

From 11 to 14, all my school mates' big clubs were either Manchester United, Chelsea, Spurs, Arsenal... and in a few instances, Leeds United.

For me, Leeds embodied everything cool, from the all-white purity of their kit to their never-say-die style of play and their unpolished under-dog tag.

I even had a Leeds United kit bag for school (in those days Brighton and Hove Albion kit bags didn't exist) and the formidable team sheet of Sprake, Reaney, Cooper, Bremner, Charlton, Hunter, Lorimer, Giles, Jones, Clarke and Gray still rolls out of my memory cells, without a second thought.

I guess my love affair with Leeds faded with puberty and by the time I went to polytechnic in Huddersfield in 1974, the glory seeking years of Don Revie had unravelled.

Yet Elland Road is another subject entirely and the fear and loathing runs deep.

I have so many bad memories of the place, including almost being maimed for life as Leeds thugs hurled house bricks following a Newcastle United v Bolton League Cup second replay in February 1976.

I had only gone along for an evening out with some Geordie mates from college.

After the game ended, we left the away end in the newly built South Stand of the ground, and remarked on the good natured and often hilarious banter with the Bolton supporters and a slightly lucky 2-1 victory.

But we had no idea what was in store for us.

We emerged from the exit gates of the stand in a crowd of many hundreds into the dark and cold night and began the slow two-mile walk to the central station and a train back to Huddersfield.

Suddenly, on my right a 20-something Newcastle fan yelled in pain, then there was another shout and another cry, mingled with screams of derision from a group of more than 30 local lads draped in Leeds United scarves. They were hurling half house bricks and assorted rubble from a bank to the right of us, where the red brick terraced housing had recently been demolished.

A guy in front of me was stumbling with bright red blood pouring from a gash on his forehead. Another man nearby was being helped to his feet after he had been felled by a piece of concrete.

I had seen football related violence before – usually at away games - but this was new and terrifying in the flickering dark with the Leeds thugs' attempts to kill or maim any random person who may be in their line of sight.

Then without any words and in a state of panic we all began to run en-masse… in any direction we could away from the rain of bricks. Eventually, after what seemed like half an hour, my mate Pete and I leapt a stone wall in the darkness, skidded on some mud and almost ended up in a canal.

We jointly breathed a sigh of relief. We were safe and later found refuge in a pub near the city station, before boarding a train back to Huddersfield.

But this was just the start of my enmity with Elland Road.

Fast forward four years to a bitterly cold Saturday 29th November 1980. Since my last brush with the backstreets of Holbeck and Armley, I had graduated with an Honours degree in History from Huddersfield Polytechnic and a post-graduate teaching certificate from nearby Bretton Hall College – ironically part of Leeds University.

I was now living in the mining village of Darton on the northern outskirts of Barnsley, teaching at a nearby high school, and I was engaged to be married.

Meanwhile, Brighton and Hove Albion were enjoying their second season in League Division One – for younger readers, this is what the Premier League used to be called.

So what better treat than to take my fiancée for a spell of Christmas shopping and her first ever football match to see my beloved Albion play "dirty" Leeds United at Elland Road.

So we hopped on the mid-morning local train and within 40 minutes we were in the city.

We stood together outside Leeds City Station, next to the Hilton Hotel, momentarily deciding whether to stop for a coffee or browse the shops which line the busy Briggate, before making our way to Elland Road.

The area outside the station concourse was particularly busy, even for a Saturday, and uniformed police officers were everywhere.

A few Brighton fans milled around us. Very few had the courage to wear blue and white, but their accents and some early morning beer gave them away instantly. We were among friends, but also the enemy.

I told my fiancée – who ironically happened to be a Geordie – not to speak too loudly.

"Let's grab a coffee," I suggested, noticing a café about 50 yards away. Then as we were about to head across the hotel forecourt to the pelican crossing, a shining black limousine suddenly pulled up alongside me.

And from behind a hotel doorman with a deep Yorkshire accent, politely said: *"Excuse me, sir."*

But before I could move aside, the rear driver's side door of the limo opened and a smiling grey-haired man alighted.

I gasped… it was Little Ern - Ernie Wise!

He was recognised instantly by a few Leeds supporters to my right. One shouted: *"Are you going to the match Ernie?"*

I stood frozen to the spot as the famous comic replied: *"Of course!"* Then trying to mimic Eric Morecambe, I spontaneously coughed: *"Arsenal!"*

I felt my face reddening, as Ernie turned with a huge grin and winked at me, before he disappeared into the hotel lobby.

My one brief moment of comic fame was gone in a cough.

But fame as they say, is brief.

A brief *"not many people know that"* factoid is that life-long Leeds United fan Ernie was born Ernest Wiseman in Bramley, a district of Leeds.

His legendary stage partner Eric was born John Eric Bartholomew in Morecambe, Lancashire.

They began performing after World War Two as Bartholomew and Wiseman, but on entering professional show business in the 1950s they discussed using the stage name of Morecambe and Leeds, but as Eric later recalled: *"We decided it sounded too much like a railway timetable"*... so Morecambe and Wise it was to be.

Anyway, back to November 1980.

After our close shave with the one with the "short, fat hairy legs" we changed plan. A coffee and a large whisky at the Whitelocks Ale House, in an alley off Briggate, was a welcome winter warmer away from the bitter cold.

There had been a few flurries of snow the day before, the temperature was hovering around minus two and out of the sunlight there were patches of frost on the ground.

"I hope you're wearing thick socks," my fiancée asked, *"My feet are freezing."*

And so we trudged around Leeds city centre doing a spot of shopping.

"Nothing too big," I urged my fiancée, *"Or they won't let us take it into the ground.*

"Oh and nothing sharp!" I added with a grin.

So just after 1pm we began the long walk towards Elland Road. In the days when the only club colours you wore to an away match might be a blue and white scarf, it was difficult to spot fellow Albion supporters. Only the occasional whisper of a Sussex accent gave our fellow travellers away.

Meanwhile, if it was at all possible, the weather had got even colder. Both of us had tucked our hands in our pockets and regretted not wearing two pairs of socks.

By 1.45pm we arrived at the ground to find huddles of our fans grouped together also trying to keep warm... and probably safe! Leeds fans were arriving in their hundreds, chanting and occasionally looking around for the enemy – us!

Just after 2pm the gates were opened and we were guided by police officers to the away enclosure. But unlike my last visit in 1976, this time it was an open caged area of the east terracing.

The crowd that day was only 14,333 (a far cry from the 35,000 plus crowds Leeds enjoyed in their Don Revie era) and I guess our motley band of supporters numbered no more than 300.

So we remained huddled and muttering between ourselves until a few braver fans began chanting *"Seagulls, Seagulls"*

It lifted our spirits as a bitter winter wind started to bite into us.

But the chanting half an hour before kick-off was a grave mistake. To our left, a growing number of Leeds fans massed on their side of the fencing, chanting abuse.

And that was when the first empty beer bottle smashed on the terracing in front of us.

The abuse grew louder and as a body of individuals, we all moved as one to our right as more bottles, coins and even a couple of darts were thrown in our direction.

A few Albion fans started to retaliate with coins and any other metal objects they could find. One blond-haired young guy picked up the darts and threw them back.

Then the police moved in on both sides of the fence making snatch arrests of anyone they deemed suspicious or caught in the act!

Welcome to Elland Road

My fiancée looked terrified, so I squeezed her hand and told her we would be okay. Now we only had the freezing temperature to worry about.

At kick-off, the abuse from the Leeds fans mellowed a little as we played 'spot the player' among their team – who were four seasons into what they would later call their "Downward Spiral". Only keeper John Lukic, Brian Greenhoff, Eddie Gray (playing left back that day) and Trevor Cherry were recognisable… oh and a certain Terry Connor, who three years later would join the Albion and spend four seasons banging in 51 goals for us.

But the match was dire… Brian Horton and Neil McNab huffed and puffed in midfield and Gerry Ryan made the odd break forward on the wing but we had very little penetration up front against Allan Clarke's well-organised side.

Then the bleakness of the day became even bleaker as Carl Harris snatched a solitary goal for Leeds.

With 15 minutes of the match remaining, my fiancée looked at me and asked: *"Can we go now?"*

Recalling the events of 1976 I thought it was a wise move to get a head start back to the city station.

So stamping our feet in an effort to find some blood circulation we – along with a couple of dozen others - made our way towards the exit.

I would not be this cold at a match for another 24 years – but that's another story!

As we moved out onto the street my fiancée said: *"I never want to go to a football match again!"*

I glanced at her and simply replied: *"Okay."*

As far as I know (we were divorced in 1990) she never did. And it would be many years before I took another partner to a Brighton game.

Leeds United sat 19th in the league that day and Allan Clarke's appointment as manager a month earlier had arrested their decline as they finished the season 9th in League Division One. But Clarke only lasted another 18 months before Eddie Gray, Peter Gunby (twice caretaker manager) and Billy Bremner all tried and failed to return the club to its glory years.

Ironically Brighton and Hove Albion finished 19th in the table. The champions in the 1980/81 season were Aston Villa.

Who Ate All the Pies? Leeds

If you go to Elland Road, the stock football food is always a pie. Sometimes with mushy peas or chips, in a paper bag, in a bowl or just wrapped in paper... but often on its own.

The one thing that differentiates Leeds and Huddersfield pies from elsewhere in the north of England is the accompaniment of *Yorkshire Relish* – a sort of cross between Worcestershire Sauce and Brown Sauce... it is simply divine!

Chapter Seven

I Will Never Live This Down
Oakwell
10 November 1981

My first house: a two-up two-down terrace in Darton on the northern outskirts of Barnsley

After graduating with a first degree from Huddersfield in 1977, I moved just 11 miles to study for a post-graduate teaching certificate at Bretton Hall College (part of Leeds University) near Barnsley.

I guess the new world of pie and peas, Sam Smith's beer and the homeliness of Yorkshire life had got under my skin. This was the land of *Last of the Summer Wine* – they even filmed an episode in the grounds of my college – and Bretton Hall was also the alma mater of the creators of *League of Gentlemen*, which may give some idea of my environs.

This part of Yorkshire was also a hotbed of league football… Leeds United, Huddersfield Town, Halifax Town, Bradford City, Barnsley, Rotherham, Doncaster Rovers and both the Sheffield clubs were all less than 21 miles away.

So by the summer of 1979, I had bought a two-up two-down terraced house and accepted a teaching job at a bustling comprehensive school in the mining village of Darton - equidistant from both Bretton Hall and Barnsley.

I lived in the village among miners and their families, and many of my pupils were the sons and daughters of miners. Most of the boys were destined to become miners themselves, and many of the girls would get jobs in businesses dependent on mining.

The sound of the local pit hooter and the rattle of coal trucks woke me early each morning and the coal dust got into my clothes and my life.

But what struck me then, and has stayed with me ever since, was the sense of community and friendship which imbued every aspect of life in that village.

If one of my charges misbehaved at school, I could be sure his or her parents would know about it, via the gossip grapevine, and he or she would be disciplined at home.

If I was ever ill in bed, a neighbour would knock at the door and ask if I needed any groceries or would leave a casserole of stew in the kitchen.

If the snow was deep, we would all help clear each others' drives and pathways.

If anyone had a party in the street, the whole street would be invited, no exceptions. And those parties were real parties with Yorkshire beer, pies, gravy, chips and puddings.

And if my fiancée had to walk home late at night, I wouldn't fear for her safety. It was a time of the greatest friendship and community I have ever known.

By happy coincidence, this was also at the start of Brighton's first full season in League Division One. But Leeds United were the only top flight Yorkshire club at this time, so local away days would be rare.

Meanwhile, as a youthful 23-year-old teacher, I immersed myself in my work. By luck, my form, who I would take through from third to fifth year, were a special bunch of kids. Full of humour and a willingness to learn, they were a real joy to teach and over the next three years a positive and disciplined bond was created.

Most of my charges came from coal mining families, so they all had a natural discipline and a hard work ethic installed from a very early age.

My bond with that class of mainly boys gave room for social chatter and joking between lessons. Usually the talk always swung back to football. All the kids were Barnsley FC fanatics, and the Tykes were an upwardly mobile club who had achieved promotion to League Division Two at the end of the 1980/81 season.

Their heroes were centre backs Mick McCarthy, player-manager Norman "Bites yer legs" Hunter, midfielder Ian Banks and former Scottish international Celtic star Ronnie Glavin. By the time the 1981/82 season was in full swing, the only thing Barnsley lacked to be able to knock on the door of League Division One was a 20 goal a season striker.

I am sure my students saw the opportunity to talk about football as an opportunity to do less written work, but from my point of view, it was always a welcome escape from the rigours of teaching them about the Black Death or the six wives of Henry VIII.

Then sometime in late October 1981, in a crescendo of excitement, my class couldn't wait to tell me of the draw for the third round of that season's League Cup.

After a well-earned 3-2 aggregate win against League Division One Swansea City (these were the days of two-leg matches in the early rounds of the cup) the Tykes had been drawn at home to the mighty Brighton and Hove Albion.

"We're gunna gob you Sir," exclaimed 15-year-old Edward, grinning from ear to ear.

"Reckon 5-0!" shouted Michael.

"And you'll never get past big Mick," added Andy.

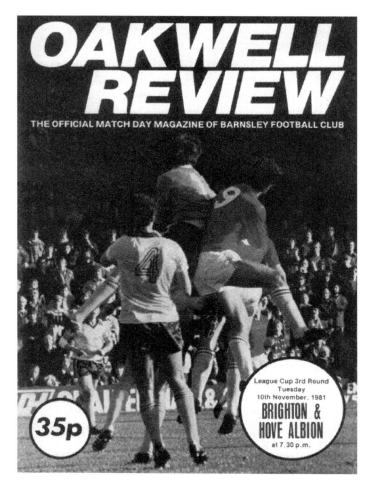

"We love McCarthy, we love McCarthy," two of the girls started chanting.

"He's gorgeous, and I'm gonna marry him," added Lucy, who always wore a red and white Mick McCarthy badge on her coat.

I can recall all their words as if it were yesterday.

"Okay, settle down now," I asserted, to howls of laughter.

The ribbing went on for at least a week while the clock ticked closer towards the match on Tuesday 10th November.

Then on the Friday before the big game two things happened in succession. First, Pete, one of the boys in the class, whose father

58

owned a large carpet business in the town shouted: *"My dad and I bet you £1 that Barnsley will win!"*

I looked at him bemused.

"Come on, meet Pete's bet, Sir!" others cheered.

I had to explain that professionally I could not bet with school kids, but I would meet the challenge with Pete's dad. So I took a £1 note out of my jacket pocket and placed it into a white envelope, on which I wrote "Brighton to win" and placed it in my desk drawer in front of the whole class.

I smiled smugly.

We were flying high in League Division One under Mike Bailey's management and sat ninth in the table. We had recently beaten Spurs and thumped Manchester City 4-1 in the league.

And while Barnsley were on a good run, they were only 5th in League Division Two and had already lost five league games.

Yes, I was confident... over confident. And I should have known better.

Then came the moment I would really regret...

"Who are you going with, Sir?" asked Michelle, a quiet girl who always sported a Princess Diana hair do. *"Bet it will be with your softy Brighton pals."*

There was silence until Andy piped up: *"The away section is shite Sir, come with us... we'll look after you when you lose."*

And to howls of laughter he added: *"And you can give Pete's dad his quid too!"*

Soon it was home time and I told my class I would think about their offer over the weekend.

Indeed, during the weekend I discovered that my next door neighbour Ernest and his 12-year-old son Richard - both die-hard Barnsley fans - were also going to the game. In a moment of decision, I agreed to go with them.

I relayed the news to my class on the Monday morning.

"Where are you standing?" at least four of my students asked.

"The west terraces," I answered to a mix of jeers and cheers.

"That's where we go too," said Andy.

"And me," added a few others.

"We'll find you Sir... my dad wants to meet you," said Pete.

"Don't worry I will see your dad at parents' evening," I rejoined, in a desperate attempt to delay the embarrassment.

The next 36 hours passed quickly and soon I was on the bus with Ernest and Richard to take the short journey to Barnsley bus station.

It was a cold and wet evening and the three of us grabbed a hot doughnut from a vendor at the bus station before walking through the backstreets of terraced housing and the smell of coke fires towards Oakwell.

The ground back in 1981 had covered South and East stands, partly covered terracing on the West side, and a vast open terrace at the North end.

The first thing I noted walking to the ground was just how many Barnsley fans there were milling all around us. We later discovered the official attendance for the game was 19,534 – a record crowd for the Tykes that season.

Suddenly Ernest nudged my arm and quietly told me to tuck my Brighton scarf well inside my jacket because the blue was *"rather obvious"*.

Soon we were queuing at the gates to the west terracing and pushing our way into the ground in a huddle of people.

The instantly recognisable NCB miners' jacket circa 1981

We had barely taken our place adjacent to the half-way line and about six rows back when a familiar voice echoed to my right: *"Eh up Sir!"* I looked across the quickly filling terrace to see 15-year-old Lucy waving madly at me. I politely waved back as another voice, this time Andy's, shouted: *"Pete and his dad are looking for you!"* I laughed and tucked my hands in my pockets as the clock ticked towards the 7.30pm kick-off.

It was a wet and miserable night, but sandwiched between hundreds of bodies and clouds of cigarette smoke, it remained warm.

I looked around me and the ground seemed almost full, except for the banked open terracing to the north (where a huge smart stand was to be built many years later for away support) where only a couple of hundred Barnsley fans were gathered.

The chanting around me grew louder when suddenly at about 7.20pm, the north end of the ground started to fill up with hundreds of what looked like identikit men all wearing black donkey jackets. As a few of them turned to chat with their friends you could see the bright fluorescent orange flashes on the back of their jackets with the letters NCB picked out in black.

"The miners have come off shift," Ernest whispered in my ear.

Barnsley was the centre of coalmining in England. In 1981 there were 56,000 miners working in the South Yorkshire coalfield and 18 operational pits in the Barnsley area.

To see all these men gathered together to loudly support their local football team was an awesome sight. But it would be the first and last time I would witness such a sight.

The national Miner's Strike of 1984/85 would change everything about Barnsley and many other areas of the UK. Part of our football and industrial past would be lost forever.

Back on the pitch, the teams were out and Mike Bailey had picked a strong line-up for this League Cup tie.

Graham Moseley was in goal and the rest of the team roll off my tongue as if it were yesterday: Shanks, Foster, Gatting, Nelson, Case, Grealish, McNab, Smith, Andy Ritchie and Michael Robinson... enough talent and experience to surely put paid to these upstarts from League Division Two.

Brighton and Hove Albion 1981/82   © The Argus

So the game kicked off, and my supposed public neutrality was to
be undone. After just two minutes in our first real attack, Steve
Gatting made a speculative shot from the edge of the penalty area
which somehow was deflected past Barnsley keeper Bobby Horn
and into the net!

The miners behind the goal were silenced, as were most of the
ground.

But while the Albion players celebrated with a small crowd of
supporters in the east stand I was jumping for joy and ripping my
scarf out of my coat on the West terracing.

Suddenly I felt a hard punch on my right shoulder and a voice said:
"Eh up lad keep it down." This was met by a dozen more groans and
expletives vented in my direction.

Ernest put his hand on my arm and firmly told me to put my scarf
away while trying to explain to a few friends that I was a "confused"
friend from the south.

The situation was diffused as I quietly panicked for my personal
safety.

Would they be so understanding if we went on to put a few more
goals past them. But I needn't have worried.

On the pitch the men in red seemed to shrug off the set-back
forcing a succession of consecutive corners and at 12 minutes the
Barnsley talisman Ronnie Glavin touched home the equaliser after a
header bounced off the post.

Mick McCarthy powers above the Albion defence to score Barnsley's second goal

The Albion responded with some slick one-touch football, but as the pitch began to chew up, we were suddenly torn to shreds.

In the 20th minute, a Barnsley corner found the head of Mick McCarthy who powered the ball into the net.

Then it went from bad to worse in the 35th minute when star striker Andy Ritchie had to be substituted after a particularly fierce tackle by Ian Banks.

Gary Stevens was an able substitute, but, like the other 10 Brighton players, was like a rabbit in the headlights as Barnsley – orchestrated by Glavin, McHale and Banks - tore into a dispirited Albion.

Two further goals from Trevor Aylott sealed our fate… a 4-1 hammering.

By the final whistle, the crowd of Barnsley fans around me had forgotten who I was, as I trooped back to the bus station and the bus home to Darton.

But the humiliation didn't end there.

In the bus station at least three of my students saw me and wasted no time in poking fun and chanting *"Barnsley, Barnsley"* in my face while another shouted: *"Call that First Division football, Sir?"*

Curious bystanders looked in my direction and laughed.

School the next day – and for the next few months – was a nightmare, as word got round the 1,400 kids at the school who often chided me over the game while passing in the corridor or playground.

I tried to keep my cool and yes, I did pay out on Pete's dad's £1 bet and learned a hard lesson about being over-confident when it comes to anything related to Brighton and Hove Albion.

Just a year later I left Barnsley for a new teaching job in rural Shropshire.

Two years ago I returned to Darton, for the first time in more than 35 years. What met me left me depressed and devastated.

In the distance the old pit heads had been replaced by rolling grassland, trees and green parkland.

To a passer-by it is picturesque… but this is nature's illusion to mask the reality.

On the main A637 a small single business park was all that had replaced a mining industry that employed thousands in Barnsley alone.

And as I strolled round the decaying remains of the village and community I once loved, everywhere I looked brought tears to my eyes. Long gone was Steve White the butchers, Broadheads the ironmongers, Henrietta's dress shop, the local newsagents, the greengrocer and the launderette - a community meeting place for the miners' wives. Below uncleaned windows and blackened limestone walls they had been replaced with a Chinese takeaway, a tanning studio, an exotic pet store, a charity shop and boarded-up facades.

And in the churchyard I found the graves of two of my former students who had both died in their early 40s.

Cars and buses passed by quickly, rarely stopping on their way to somewhere else.

Only the elderly trundle along the pavement, past shops where there is nothing left to buy; walking small dogs and faces waxing grey and etched in lines of worry.

It reminded me of scenes I also witnessed in Northumberland (where my paternal grandfather and great grandfather were both miners) where three generations of families have been unemployed since 1984.

Their former pit communities have crumbled into decay, with all manner of social problems: derelict housing, rotting schools, drug dependency, street crime, high rates of teenage suicide and homelessness.

But on a personal and positive note, more than 37 years after that barnstorming football match in 1981 I have remained good friends with two of those mouthy 15-year-old students. Andy (who stayed close to where he was born) and Edward (who moved away to Cornwall) are now both in their 50s with kids of their own and still like to remind me of that night at Oakwell, especially after a beer or two of old time reminiscences.

I knew I would never live that match down.

As for the Albion, the team recovered quickly from the 4-1 humiliation, chalking up impressive victories against Sunderland, Southampton and West Ham over the next few weeks.

Brighton and Hove Albion finished the 1981/82 season in a respectable 13th position in League Division One with 52 points. The champions that season were Liverpool.
Barnsley finished their season in 10th place in League Division Two.

Who Ate All the Pies? Barnsley

If you think of food associated with Barnsley you'll no doubt
think of Barnsley chops. But they are not exactly football grub.
I have lived in Huddersfield, Leeds and Barnsley and nowhere
does a Pie Floater better than at Oakwell. It is simply a hot
pork pie floating in a bowl of mushy peas, with a generous
dollop of either red or brown sauce. Gorgeous!

Chapter Eight

And Outterside Must Score
Ludlow
21 May 1983

A 1983 Cup Final rosette   © Bob Hobden

How does someone who claims to be a lifelong Brighton and Hove Albion die-hard fan excuse not being at Wembley when his club reached its only FA Cup Final in history?

Well, I am sure I can knit a good few excuses into this chapter, but that does not stop 21st May 1983 being the biggest personal regret in all my years following the Albion.

A year earlier I had moved south to the sleepy market town of Ludlow in Shropshire to start a new teaching job. I had also recently married, bought our first proper home together, started furnishing that house on one salary, passed my driving test, bought my first car and we had begun trying for our first child. It was a typical life situation for many people of our age in the early 1980s. We were skint but happy, with our eyes focussed on the future.

The tranquil Ludlow Cricket Club in south Shropshire

Outside of work we began to get to know new friends and started picking up the local dialect, which at times seemed almost mediaeval and amusing in the same breath. But while trying to fit in to these new environs, I could not bring myself to call dating a woman "wenching" or to refer to a girlfriend as an "owd wench" or my mum and dad as "towd mon and umman." It really was a place lost in a previous time.

Yes, Ludlow was as different from Sussex or Yorkshire as you could imagine.

But the town had a fabulous cricket club so I was able to pursue my summer passion for the game on a weekly basis, with nets on Wednesday evenings and games each Saturday.

My sometime wayward off-spin and middle order batting had allowed me to claim a place in the second and third XIs, depending who was fit and available to play. But I was practising my bowling hard and was desperate to breakthrough to the Ludlow first team. On Saturday 14th May I had enjoyed a memorable Second XI game away at Ruyton XI Towns near Shrewbury, where I had taken two wickets and three catches – including a spectacular diving one at Silly Point. My ego was boosted and my hopes were high. Meanwhile, like every other Brighton and Hove Albion fan, I had been following the fortunes of my team's cup run and the paradoxically dire league form via *Match of the Day*, *Sports Report* and forays to nearby away matches.

A 3-0 humiliation at Stoke City's Victoria Ground the previous October, a 2-0 defeat at Coventry City's Highfield Road and a narrow 1-0 loss at Villa Park stay in the memory, as does a wonderful 4-0 thumping of Manchester City in the fourth round of the FA Cup at the end of January – my only visit to the Goldstone Ground that season.

So on Saturday 16th April, at the start of the cricket season, the Albion had just beaten Sheffield Wednesday 2-1 at Highbury in the Semi-Final of the FA Cup in front of 54,000 delirious fans, thanks to brilliant goals from Jimmy Case and Michael Robinson. But we were also rooted to the bottom of League Division One with just 35 points from 36 games.

From a league perspective manager Jimmy Melia's expansive football was often fun to watch, but with 62 goals conceded and a goal difference of minus 28, with still six games to play, relegation was a real danger.

At least we were into our first ever FA Cup Final.

And I was to miss it!

This is partly explained by where my life was at back in the summer of 1983, but also by the fact that in the days before mobile phones and the Internet, there were only three ways to get tickets for an FA Cup Final: either by queuing at your club's ticket office, by making a written application with a crossed cheque included or by a pleading phone call. I failed at each option.

So I was determined to watch the final live on BBC TV in the comfort of my own living room…until fate intervened.

After the routine net session at Ludlow Cricket Club, the captain of the Second XI introduced me to the First XI skipper. A huge smile spread across my face when he then told me I was in the twelve for the home game against Wem on Saturday!

"Wow, thanks," were about my only words of reply.

"Your off-spin may give us some options, as Greg (the club's first choice spinner) *is away on holiday,"* the captain explained.

As the news sank in, my joy was tempered when I realised the game would clash with the FA Cup Final.

By 8am on the Saturday morning I was sat in front of our TV watching the live build-up to the final with my heart torn. Next to the sofa was a kit bag with my box, thigh pad and cricket whites inside, washed and neatly ironed. Leaning against the chair was my bagged Gray-Nicolls bat.

The rest of the morning passed in a blur.

The Twin Towers of Wembley in May 1983   © **Steve Tennyson**

Then after a light lunch of cheese and salad, I was packing my car to make the short two mile drive to the cricket ground.

The game was due to start at 2pm and I was gradually introduced to the rest of the first team squad – most of whom I had never met before, or I had only seen in passing.

I presumed I was to be 12th man and therefore to be left in the pavilion for the game, but that was progress to me, plus I could listen to the Final on the radio!

But 20 minutes after arriving, the team was announced... I was playing and down to bat at number 8 or 9.

I am unsure whether anyone else heard it, but a retiring 27-year-old school teacher in the corner of the dressing room made a sharp intake of breath and a semi silent *"whoop"*. I was with the big boys at last!

At 1.50pm, the umpire tossed a coin and we waited in the warm sunshine of the pavilion steps for the result... we were bowling first! The match started promptly and I was dispatched to field at Extra Cover. I wanted to be closer to the bat, but hey-ho, it didn't really matter because I was playing in the first team.

Meanwhile, in my parked car, the radio was tuned to BBC Radio 2, and on the field I relaxed in the knowledge that the Cup Final wouldn't kick off for another hour.

The teams emerge for the 1983 FA Cup Final   © Steve Tennyson

But the Albion team – minus the suspended skipper Steve Foster – was probably the best we could field: Graham Moseley in goal and in front of him Chris Ramsey, Graham Pearce, Steve Howlett, Steve Gatting, Tony Grealish, Gary Stevens, Jimmy Case, Neil Smillie, Gordon Smith, and our star striker Michael Robinson.

Gordon Smith celebrates after heading the Albion ahead early in the first half

Around 3pm, looking out of my car window, Wem had accrued 70 runs for the loss of only two wickets and we were on to our third change of bowlers.

I hoped for my turn to bowl and remained outwardly keen… but I was never chosen. I guess the captain didn't want to take a risk while Wem were steadily amassing runs.

By 3.15pm the visitors were starting to accelerate the score and I was standing at deep Third Man totally unaware that 148 miles away at Wembley, a Gordon Smith header had just put Brighton ahead.

I was equally unaware almost an hour later, with Wem bowled out for 172 that Frank Stapleton had equalised for Manchester United. So as we trooped in for tea at 4.10pm I had taken one catch at Mid-Wicket and the Cup Final was all square at 1-1.

I then grabbed a cup of tea and excused myself from my team-mates and sat in my car to listen to the action from Wembley... it was riveting.

As our captain called our team together to prepare to bat, I sheepishly asked permission to sit in my car, explaining that I was a Brighton and Hove Albion fan.

He laughed in reply.

"Why aren't you down at Wembley?" he asked quizzically. *"Yes, of course, sit and listen, but make sure you are padded up and ready when we lose our fifth wicket,"* he added.

I grinned and ran back to the car and the radio.

Brighton were playing superbly, but at 72 minutes a wonder goal from outside the box by Ray Wilkins put Manchester United ahead. Time was running out... in Ludlow we were already two wickets down with less than 20 on the board.

But at Wembley with four minutes of normal time to go, Tony Grealish found Gary Stevens in the penalty area and the marauding defender steered the ball into the United net to make the score 2-2 and force extra time.

Many years later Gary Stevens recalls the game as being the biggest match of his life.

"The atmosphere; the fans and the banners stand out in my mind," he said.

"I remember it was late in the game and we were 2-1 behind, which was a bit harsh on us, when we won a corner. I hadn't scored a goal all season and I wasn't even going up for corners at that point.

"I can remember looking across to the dug-out where Jimmy Melia and suspended skipper Steve Foster were waving at me to get up the park. I went forward and Jimmy Case knocked the ball to the edge of the area from the corner. I'm not sure whether Tony Grealish was trying to pick out a pass or whether it was a shot, but I don't think he struck the ball as well as he would have liked. I was running in with a view of hitting a shot and the ball fell perfectly at my feet. I took one touch to control it and then hit it as hard as I

could towards the target. I struck the ball really cleanly and it did exactly what I intended – beat United's Gary Bailey and hit the back of the net!"

As extra time at Wembley began, back in Ludlow our third wicket fell, but my ears were still glued to the radio. I could scarcely believe that we were not only holding Manchester United, but actually outplaying them.

Then with 10 minutes of extra time to go, someone knocked on my driver's car window. *"Nic, get padded up, you're going in at nine,"* said one of our senior players. *"How's the Cup Final going?"*

I explained briefly the run of the game and quickly made my way to the pavilion to put on my pads and box and collect my bat.

My mind was in North London as at about 5.30pm I walked out to the middle to bat.

I glanced at the scoreboard… we were a paltry 78 for 8 and down among the tail… and as I passed the other batsman he patted me on the shoulder and quipped: *"We just need to score more runs Nic… just stay with me."* I smiled and took a middle and leg guard.

Meanwhile at Wembley… there's a minute to go and the players are on their last legs, many seemingly settling for the replay.

Wilkins, shinpads discarded, passes to Kevin Moran who strikes a somewhat aimless ball up field. It's cut out on the volley by Stevens who finds Jimmy Case.

In one movement our midfield maestro controls the ball, turns and then lobs it over the United defence, which has been caught square.

Michael Robinson meets the lob and slides the ball across to his right and Gordon Smith, who is clear with only the keeper to beat.

Destiny awaits and beyond my ears on BBC Radio Two commentator Peter Jones, cries: *"And Smith must score!"*

But United keeper Gary Bailey smothers his poor shot and the course of Brighton and Hove Albion history is changed forever.

Back in Ludlow I faced the first testing ball from Wem's senior leg-spinner, who suddenly appeared like a ghost from behind the umpire to whizz in a quick ball. I lunged forward with a straight bat, but the ball fizzed past the outside edge and was taken by the keeper wide of my off-stump.

A minute later his second ball was floated up some 10mph slower than the first, I tried to push forward but over reached myself and my aimless defence was undone as the ball found the edge of my bat and nestled behind me in the keeper's gloves.

I trudged back to the pavilion slowly with dismal debut figures of facing two balls for a duck.

I am still unsure whether my emotions that afternoon matched that of Gordon Smith.

Many years later Smith gave a media interview on that day in May 1983.

"It rankles with me that I could have won the FA Cup for Brighton. I still feel bad," he said. *"Three years after the final, I'd signed for Manchester City and we'd gone to Malaysia on tour. I was in the middle of Kuala Lumpur and a young boy was collecting players' autographs.*

"After I signed his book he stared at my signature and said, 'Oh, you are Gordon Smith. How did you miss in the Cup Final?"

The scoreboard at half time shows Albion leading 1-0 with Gordon Smith the scorer   © Steve Tennyson

I guess the significance of that day in May 1983 was quite different for the two of us… I was never chosen to play for First XI cricket ever again and spent my life quietly forgetting it. Poor Gordon is still reminded of that moment at Wembley 36 years later!

For the purists out there: for the replay on the following Thursday, Manchester United were unchanged, while we welcomed back captain Steve Foster (who had been suspended for the Cup Final) and played Steve Gatting at right-back for the injured Chris Ramsey. United had learned their lesson and 4-0 was the biggest Cup Final margin since 1903 (Bury 6, Derby 0).

Two goals in five minutes midway through the first half - by Bryan Robson and then the youngest Cup Final scorer, Norman Whiteside, just 18 - put them beyond reach.

Memories, now just faded memories   © The Daily Mirror

Robson scored a close range third goal before halftime, and Arnold Muhren completed the scoring from the penalty spot. United and Robson were to collect the Cup twice more in the next seven seasons.

As a personal aside, a year before the Cup Final, in 1982, Gordon Smith paid a public relations visit on behalf of the club to Tollbridge House in Shoreham-by-Sea – a residential home for the elderly, where my maternal grandmother lived her last couple of years. He was photographed outside the home with a number of residents and his arm around my granny.

My grandmother died a year later in May 1984.

I kept the photo of her and Gordon Smith for many years, but as I came to gather material for this book, I could not find it anywhere. I guess that forgetfulness is the last refuge of the defeated.

Brighton and Hove Albion lost the FA Cup Final and were relegated from League Division One at the end of the 1982/83 season in 22nd place with 40 points. Champions that season were Liverpool, with Watford as runners-up.

Who Ate All the Pies? Ludlow

Ludlow is a thriving market town based around the area's cattle and sheep farming. It has a long history of brewing, but the last brewery in town, the Ludlow and Craven Arms Brewery, shut up shop in the 1930s. Then in 2006 the Ludlow Brewing Company began making its own array of craft beers and real ales. And a good beer needs a good pie, and Ludlow is a place where you can sample the most amazing steak pies you will ever taste... ideal for watching football on the telly!

Chapter Nine

Get a Lorra That Lawro
The Goldstone Ground
28 January 1984

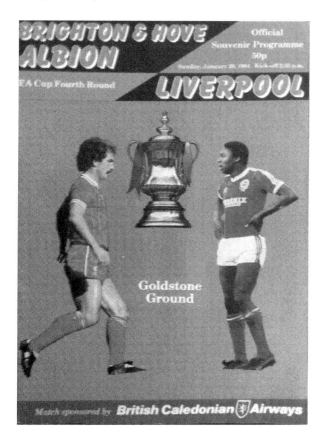

There are few, if any, Albion players who have gone on to TV celebrity status after hanging up their boots quite like Mark "Lawro" Lawrenson.

Even if the former Ireland international (only Irish by virtue of his grandfather) does mention his home town team of Preston and his glory years at Liverpool in his broadcasts far more often than reflecting on the 152 appearances he made for Brighton and Hove Albion (1977/81), he is, and always will, be an Albion legend.

Mark was born in Penwortham and attended Preston Catholic College, a Jesuit school. His father, Tom, had been a winger for Preston North End. He always wanted to be a footballer, although his mother, Theresa, wanted him to become a priest.

He began his career in 1974, as a 17-year-old, with his hometown club Preston North End, who were then managed by World Cup winner Bobby Charlton. Lawrenson was voted Preston's Player of the Year for the 1976/77 season.

But then after 73 league appearances for the Deepdale club, he moved to Alan Mullery's Brighton and Hove Albion in the summer before the start of the 1977/78 season for £100,000.

Ironically, the Albion had outbid Liverpool, who also showed interest in the 19-year-old Lawrenson. The young defender made his Brighton debut on 20th August 1977 in a 1–1 draw against Southampton at The Dell.

He settled in well at the Goldstone Ground and made 40 league appearances by the end of his first season at the club, both in central defence and at full-back. His style of playing out of defence and his keen positioning endeared him to the Albion faithful.

But when the club entered a financial crisis in 1981, Lawrenson was forced to leave to make funds available.

A number of other clubs were interested in signing him, but it was Liverpool manager Bob Paisley who finally secured his signature. Liverpool offered a club transfer record of £900,000, and Lawrenson joined in the summer of 1981. He was to form a formidable central defensive partnership with Alan Hansen, after Phil Thompson suffered an injury and fell out of favour.

The Albion in return secured the services of Liverpool midfield legend Jimmy Case, who over the next four seasons was to become a club legend in his own right.

Case joined Brighton in August 1981 as a £450,000 makeweight for the Lawrenson transfer and he played a large part in the success achieved at the Goldstone Ground in the early 1980s. When the Albion were relegated from League Division One in 1983, Case showed true loyalty and remained at the Goldstone Ground for nearly two more years.

Nothing embodies the link between 18 times Champions and five times European champions Liverpool and little old Brighton and Hove Albion more than Case and Lawrenson.

Yet by the January of 1984 (just eight months after our FA Cup Final defeat to Manchester United) we had beaten that season's European Champions twice at Anfield in the previous two seasons. We were quickly becoming Liverpool's bogey team.

So when we were drawn at home in the 4th round of the 1984 FA Cup against a Liverpool team that included such legends as Phil Neal, Mark Lawrenson, Graeme Souness, former Seagull Michael Robinson and Ian Rush (who would finish that season with 47 goals), the squeaky bums were not in Sussex, but 220 miles away in the L4 post code area.

The game was scheduled for Sunday 29th January, and after the personal debacle of our FA Cup Final the previous May, I was not going to miss this fixture for anything. Even with my wife expecting our first child in early June, I knew I had to be at the Goldstone for this game.

So after driving down to Sussex and back in my old green Saab, breaking down twice on the journey in foul January weather, I managed to secure my ticket for the game.

The day itself was something very special.

Liverpool had already thrashed Newcastle United by 4-0 in the third round of the Cup, but I had a feeling that we could sneak a win.

I drove back down from Ludlow to Sussex on the Saturday and stayed with my maternal grandmother in Shoreham for the weekend.

At the time I did not know that this would be the last time I would see my sweet gran, who would die suddenly of a stroke on the steps of her Tollbridge House home just three months later.

As I write this, the personal poignancy of that FA Cup tie grows 100 fold.

But back on that Sunday morning, buoyed by my grandmother's fried breakfast of eggs, bacon, sausages and toast, I drove the seven short miles to the Goldstone Ground, before finding off-street parking south of the ground near where the old Clarks bakery once stood.

As I got out of the car I immediately felt there a buzz in the air. It was cold but the atmosphere was warmed by the noise of the Goldstone.

Despite languishing 10th in League Division Two and the glory days of the top flight well behind us, there really was a cup fever about the place, with chants of *"Seagulls, Seagulls"* at every turn.

This was also an historic day for the club and for televised football. It was the first time the Goldstone Ground had hosted a Sunday FA Cup match, and it was a live television debut for the stadium.

It was also the first time a second tier club had been shown live outside of an FA Cup Final.

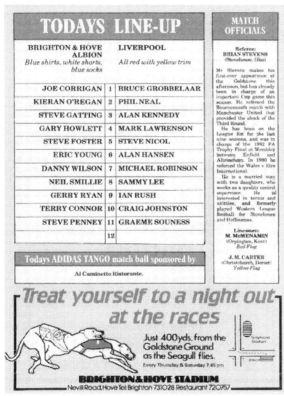

The team line-ups that day in 1984

82

So with my match ticket clasped tightly in my hand I made my way through the turnstiles to my normal spot in the North Stand – a similar spot to the one I had occupied at my very first game almost 17 years earlier.

The rest, as they say, is history.

On paper, our team that day, in front of 19,057 fans, seemed a pale shadow of the ones which had graced the League Division One for the previous four seasons... no Peter Ward, no Brian Horton nor Andy Ritchie. No Jimmy Case (suspended), no Gary Stevens, no Michael Robinson and no Gordon Smith.

Instead, in front of an ageing Joe Corrigan in goal were: Chris Hutchings, Steve Gatting, Tony Grealish, Steve Foster, Alan Young, Danny Wilson, Neil Smillie, Gerry Ryan, Terry Connor and Steve Penney. The team had a certain second tier air about it.

Although we were a division apart and clear underdogs, the Albion made the better start of the two sides. The Albion's front four used their pace to good effect and pinned Liverpool back for much of the first half.

Then a stroke of luck as Liverpool captain Graeme Souness was forced off early with a hamstring injury, which seemed to boost the Albion's confidence.

But we had to be alert and most eyes were not only on our players but also on the Liverpool danger men.

Ian Rush had a golden chance right on 45 minutes when he was thwarted first by Corrigan and then the rebound was blocked on the line superbly by Steve Foster.

The breakthrough was yet to come as the half time whistle blew but Liverpool were looking more and more dangerous.

The North Stand was making one hell of a noise and over half time most of us were happy that we were holding the game.

The match livened up in the second half as the sun shone down over a full Goldstone Ground.

We started strongly and with pace across the pitch and it took just 12 minutes before Gerry Ryan was put clear by Tony Grealish behind the Liverpool defence and brilliantly chipped the ball over Grobbelaar to break the deadlock.

There was pandemonium all around me and I had at least one Bovril spilled down my jeans and something resembling squashed bread and cheese smeared over the back of my anorak.

"We're fucking leading… come on you Albion," a guy next to me screamed.

And in front of me, a young boy, resembling me all those years ago, turned to his dad and asked: *"Who scored?"*

Then just over a minute later Terry Connor – who I had seen play in a Leeds United shirt just four years earlier - was sent through, beat the offside trap and shot past the keeper from outside the penalty area to shock Liverpool and make it 2-0.

Gerry Ryan puts the Albion ahead   © **The Argus**

As I write this, I am searching my thesaurus in a vain for a word which means more than pandemonium, because the maelstrom of chaos that followed the first goal was doubled following the second. And the little boy in front of me naively asked his dad: *"Have we scored again?"*

The Albion were through to the 5th Round of the FA Cup once more. All around me our fans were running through an extended and wild repertoire of Albion chants and songs and hero worshipping of our players and manager.

84

Everyone seemed to be hugging everyone else in ways reminiscent of our promotion victory at St James Park five years earlier.
It remains as one of the greatest Albion games I have ever witnessed.

Gerry Ryan, who also scored against Liverpool in the FA Cup the previous season, immediately after the game ended said: *"It's unbelievable. To beat the best team in Europe twice in the FA Cup is magnificent, but to score on both occasions really puts the icing on the cake for me. I'll never forget it.*

"The goal at Liverpool last season was a simple tap-in after some great work by Michael Robinson.

"But my effort today was more spectacular, although I thought the referee was going to blow for offside when Tony Grealish lobbed the ball over the heads of Mark Lawrenson and Alan Hansen.

"Fortunately, Phil Neal had played me on so I raced towards the penalty area and struck the ball past Bruce Grobbelaar."

Gerry admitted that the early departure of Liverpool skipper Graeme Souness with a hamstring injury had a big bearing on the result.

"Graeme is a major influence on the side and his loss unsettled them," he said.

"Even though we've beaten them twice in the last year, I still regard them as the best. I thoroughly expect them to finish the season as League Champions and European Cup holders."

Jimmy Case added: *"This has to be an even greater achievement than when we knocked them out of the Cup last season.*

"People might have thought us lucky last time but this proved it was no fluke. The lads were really keyed up and it was a really great all-round team performance.

"Against a team like Liverpool, every player has to be on top form and, on this occasion, everyone played their part.

"It was certainly one of our best performances of the season."

The Albion's new manager Chris Cattlin added: *"Our players beat Liverpool for pace. Joe Corrigan did extremely well in goal and you couldn't fault our back four.*

"I watched Liverpool two or three times prior to this game. Teams lose to them through fear. I made sure that wouldn't happen to us.

"We have beaten the best side in Europe and beaten them fair and square."

Extracting myself from the milling masses I eventually found my way back to my car, and intoxicated purely by exhilaration I drove happily the short distance back to my grandmother's flat, a fish and chip tea and a bottle of beer waiting for me.

The next morning I kissed her cheek goodbye.

That final kiss and that FA Cup tie remain with me to this day.

Brighton and Hove Albion finished the 1983/84 season in League Division Two in 9th place on 60 points. Champions that year were Chelsea on 88 points and runners-up on goal difference were Sheffield Wednesday.

Our FA Cup run ended in the 5th Round with a 3-1 defeat to Watford at Vicarage Road.

Liverpool ended the season as League Division One champions, League Cup winners and European Cup winners. The only trophy that evaded them was the FA Cup thanks to Brighton and Hove Albion.

Who Ate All the Pies? Liverpool

In every pub and café around Anfield and Goodison you will always get a bowl of this superfood: Scouse – or lobscouse as it was originally called.

It is an amazing beef or lamb stew with carrots and vegetables and thought to originate from the sailors who stopped in the docks of the city. Similar to Lancashire and Mancunian Hot Pot, but scousers will argue otherwise.

Every place has its own recipe, so best to try it twice!

Chapter Ten

Fans with Typewriters and Teletext
Scotland
1990-2001

The Scotsman building, North Bridge, Edinburgh

In the summer of 1973, John Lennon and Yoko Ono's marriage was on the rocks. As an unusual remedy, Ono suggested that Lennon embark on an affair with their assistant, May Pang.
That decision led to Lennon's *"Lost Weekend,"* the 18 months that the ex-Beatle lived with Pang in her New York apartment and a rented home in Los Angeles.

Musically, it was a productive time in Lennon's career. He completed three albums – *Mind Games, Walls and Bridges* and *Rock 'n' Roll* – and produced LPs for Ringo Starr and Harry Nilsson.

In no way am I comparing myself with John Lennon, but my own *"Lost Weekend"* was something similar… but one hell of a lot longer! My 11 full years living and working as a newspaper journalist in Scotland was filled with a divorce, a marriage, two children, five house moves, six jobs, another divorce and a raft of national press awards during the most productive and unforgettable period of my life.

But it was also a complete exile from my home of Sussex and my on-going love affair with Brighton and Hove Albion.

The last game before my move north of the border in October 1990 was a 2-1 victory at Ewood Park against Blackburn Rovers on 29th September.

Although our glory years in League Division One were well behind us, few could have predicted the dark days which lay ahead.

Meanwhile, my exile to Scotland brought an unexpected football related surprise.

I was driving north in my sporty Fiat Uno Turbo on the M6 on a bright October day to begin my new life, when suddenly, just north of Penrith, I was overtaken at high speed by a gold coloured BMW 6 series.

The rogue car must have been travelling at about 90mph, and two things struck me: the driver was steering one-handed while using his brick of a mobile phone, and the car registration was a striking TB1. I continued on my way and thought no more of my over-taker. But about 35 miles further on in my journey as I crossed onto the M74, I came across the same car near Ecclefechan.

This time the driver was travelling at a more sedate 40mph in the slow lane. I noticed he was still deep in conversation on his mobile phone.

As I overtook the BMW, I glanced and immediately recognised the driver's face… it was Terry Butcher, the former England and Rangers captain – hence TB1. Five miles further on, TB overtook me again!

Two days later the national media announced that Terry had quit Rangers to become player/manager of League Division 1 club Coventry City. I guess the guy had some negotiating to do on the day our paths crossed.

Within six months of arriving in Scotland I bought an old and derelict stone built lodge house in Argyll, alongside Loch Fyne - bordered on the west by the wild North Atlantic Ocean - and began the joyous task of renovating it into a dream home.

With three dogs, swarms of blood-sucking midges and a new partner beside me it would become an experience I will never forget. It was made all the more special by the wildlife that surrounded us. Sixty-two species of mammal live wild in and around Scotland and it soon seemed that most of them lived near me.

My first home in Scotland near Tarbert, Argyll. The eagle-eyed reader may notice a satellite dish on the cottage – something which was not available in 1990.

In the late summer of 1991, while driving along the winding gorse-lined road to Kilberry, on the Knapdale headland, I braked suddenly as a rabbit ran at speed towards me... chased by a dark brown cat. The rabbit darted into the undergrowth at the side of the road, while the cat stopped in its tracks and quickly perched on its hind legs sniffing the summer air.

A sharp pointed nose and cream coloured underbelly betrayed its real identity. This was no cat, but an adult Pine Marten – probably the most wonderful creature I ever seen in the wild.

As the sun played on its face and sparkling eyes, an image was lodged which has never left me.

But something much rarer was in store. The shy Scottish Wild Cat is considered at serious risk of extinction, due to a lack of protected habitat. But that didn't stop one such male Wild Cat stealing our dogs' food for more than a fortnight during the winter of 1991. Until tragically one night the magnificent creature was run over and killed by a passing vehicle on the A83, which ran alongside our cottage. It was indeed a different world to anything I was used to. Scottish football was equally diverse and different from English football, as I was soon to discover.

An attendance of 900 to watch a local derby Scottish League game between Ayr United and Kilmarnock was considered a bumper gate! But it was also fun as you got to talk with the players and even meet them for the odd pint after a game.

So I bade my time with so-called substitute football... not watching substitutes but going to as many Scottish league games as I could manage.

Over the next 10 years, I visited at least 30 different league grounds, watched four promotion clinching games, befriended three club chairmen and interviewed dozens of players and managers. I also saw an ambulance drive onto the pitch at Stair Park (Stranraer's ground) to save the life of a goalkeeper, chased a stray dog around Links Park (Montrose's ground) and watched as sheets of corrugated iron fell from the grandstand roof at Ochilview (Stenhousemuir).

But the highlight of those substitute games was probably watching an Albion Rovers winger lob Peterhead's then-teenage goalkeeper from the half way line at Balmoor Stadium, with the help of a wind assistance of at least 50mph!

I also managed to get to a handful of Scottish top flight games during those years.

But the most memorable by some distance was taking my eldest son Ben to watch Hibernian play Kilmarnock at Easter Road on a wet August Saturday in 1997.

Hibernian won the game 4-0, and to this day it is the only match I have ever attended where I missed all four goals being scored!

We drove to the game in Leith, but due to Edinburgh Festival traffic we took ages to get parked. When we eventually reached the turnstile we heard a roar as Hibs scored their first goal. Four minutes later, we were asking other fans for details of the goal. Some 20 minutes into the game, my then 12-year-old son asked if he could get a pie and a drink. I accompanied him to the refreshment counter under the west stand. As we were ordering his food we heard another huge roar as Hibs scored their second goal on 24 minutes.

Then midway through the second half Ben needed to use the toilets and as a diligent father I also accompanied him to the urinals... and yes we missed what was by all accounts a blinder of an own goal, as Hibs went 3-0 up.

With my son quickly losing all interest in Scottish football, our humiliation was complete after we left at 90 minutes to avoid the Festival and football traffic... we were passing through the exit gates as Pat McGinlay scored Hibs fourth goal.

And just to think we could have driven 220 miles south to see my beloved Brighton and Hove Albion humbled 2-1 to lowly Scarborough!

The real football highlight of my time in Scotland was getting to interview England legend Paul Gascoigne on the day he signed for Glasgow Rangers.

By the summer of 1995, the Gateshead born Geordie had enjoyed three years playing for top Italian side Lazio.

It was no secret that although he enjoyed immense success on the pitch, he found the Italian language a little tricky.

Many football punters tipped him to return to England and maybe re-sign for Spurs, Manchester United or even his home team Newcastle United.

So his transfer to Rangers for £4.3 million that summer shocked everyone.

On the July day his transfer was to be formally announced to the media, I had been tasked by my news desk at the *Glasgow Herald* to attend a Rangers training session and then a press conference at Ibrox to try and grab a word with the great player.

The blond-haired Gazza at his first training session with his new Rangers team-mates, prior to signing for the club in 1995

So I spent an hour with my photographer watching a lithe, tanned and fit Gazza train with his team-mates we made our way to Glasgow G51.

The stadium was mobbed by Rangers fans daubed in blue and white, and some with orange sashes, hoping to get a glimpse of their new hero.

I picked my way through the crowd, past a cordon of police officers and showed my press pass at the players' entrance.

Once inside, the assembled press pack was treated to prawn sandwiches, croissants and coffee before being ushered into a bustling meeting room.

Rangers' manager Walter Smith and club chairman David Murray sat at the top table next to their new superstar.

The formal press conference lasted about 35 minutes before we were led out pitch side for a photo opportunity.

Gazza was beaming and in a playful mood with us all.

I had not yet managed to ask him a question so waited for my moment. And it wasn't long before the chance came.

It had crossed my mind that if this Geordie had found the Italian language difficult to deal with, how would he manage broad Glaswegian?

So as Gazza sat in the stands for a final picture opportunity - and remembering my own Tyneside roots – I asked him: *"Do you think you will cope with the language here, Paul?"*

Quick as a flash, he turned to me and replied: *"Whey aye man, dyer think thaal understand me. Ye knaa what ah mean leik."*

Both of us broke into a loud chuckle.

Twenty minutes later as we made our way out of the stadium, one of my colleagues asked: *"What did Gazza say to you?"*

I shrugged and lied: *"Didn't understand a word!"*

Scotland was a whole new world of football and as far from the beauty of the English game as I ever thought possible.

In the meantime, I still managed the odd journey south for a few League Division 2 and 3 games whenever Brighton played anywhere like Darlington, Carlisle or Hartlepool… but these were frustrating years for me.

These were also the years largely before the Internet or digital mobile phones, and I had to wait until 1999 to discover the North Stand Chat forum.

My first two years living and working in the wild in the beautiful north-west of Argyll were the most life changing.

I could sit for hours watching otters or Atlantic seals splashing around in the loch outside my back door and forget about life, work and even football.

There was no TV reception at all and I relied wholly for news of the Albion on national radio… in this case on **Sports Report** on a Saturday on BBC Radio 5.

```
MONDAY RESULTS                        1/2
NATIONWIDE LEAGUE
Division Three
Brighton         0-2 Southend     6,503
Cardiff          6-1 Exeter       9,038
Scunthorpe       2-2 Macclesfield 3,168
Shrewsbury       3-2 Barnet       2,991
Torquay          1-1 Kidd'minster 2,467

Darlington       OFF Rochdale
Halifax          OFF Carlisle
Hartlepool       OFF Lincoln
Hull             OFF Blackpool
Leyton O       · OFF Plymouth
Mansfield        OFF Cheltenham
York             OFF Chesterfield

Celtic visit Shelbourne in a pre-season
friendly on Saturday while Limerick
play host to Chelsea. Both matches
kick-off at 7pm.

Brighton leading scorer Mike Small has
had talks with Chelsea and is thinking
over a possible move.

Port Vale new signing Martin Foyle will
make his debut on Sunday in a
pre-season friendly against non-league
Newcastle Town at Lyme Valley Parkway
stadium - kick-off 2.30.

 302 Football 320 General 340 Cricket
 350 Latest    360 Racing  380 M/Sport
Next Page Football    Cricket    Latest
```

The Godsend of Teletext and Ceefax

The rolling news and sports of Radio 5 Live wasn't born until 1994!
So even our 3-1 League Division Two play-off final defeat to Notts
County was a matter of picking up the left-overs and scraps from
the game from the back pages of that Monday's *Glasgow Herald*
and the *Daily Record*.

Matters improved a little when I moved to the gentler environs of
Galloway in 1992, but like most other BHAFC exiles of that time, I
still survived on newspaper reports, Grandstand, BBC radio and the
Godsend of Teletext and Ceefax… the onscreen TV news updates
which appeared in turquoise and white pixels stolen from Pacman.
Civilisation slowly caught up with me and in 1994 I moved again,
this time to national daily newspaper *The Scotsman* in Edinburgh.

During the ensuing few years I felt lucky as I was surrounded by football-daft workmates and we would spend a lot of our time between jobs talking about our passion for the game.

While some of our colleagues were crafting timeless back page headlines such as *Super Caley Go Ballistic Celtic Are Atrocious* and the sublime *Emerson Late and Linked with Parma* we recreated the support for our clubs by other means... usually by staring at Teletext live reports of games waiting for goals and news of bookings and sending-offs or the latest transfer news or matches postponed. And then waiting for the league tables to update as the matches ended. Sometimes we had to wait until the next day for full updates to appear on screen.

Work was often punctuated by a loud cheer from across the newsroom as a reporter had just seen that his team had scored! Or by an even louder *"fuck it"* if a team had conceded a last minute goal or had a player sent off.

Our passion was at times consuming.

The urinals in the North Stand at The Goldstone Ground circa 1997
© Chris Stratton

John Penman, the deputy news editor at **The Scotsman** even began a weekly column titled *Fans with Typewriters* where he asked for readers to submit their most amusing football related stories.

One *Fans With Typewriters* topic became almost viral when John asked readers how best to create the atmosphere and reality of a game when as a supporter you are stuck at home or work and can't get to the match.

The result, following numerous letters from readers and fellow journos, was both timeless and hilarious.

The 12 point guidelines went something like this:

1 Switch on the Ceefax football pages on your TV
2 Ensure you are stocked up with at least two dozen cans of Tennents' Lager
3 Invite a couple of your best football mad pals to join you
4 Begin drinking the lager at least two hours before kick-off
5 Ensure that no-one flushes the toilet
6 Leave the toilet door open
7 Make three mugs of luke-warm Bovril in plastic cups for half time
8 Ask your wife and her friends to walk in front of the TV whenever they want
9 Buy your child a whistle and invite him/her to blow it whenever they want
10 Ensure that one of your pals suffers from Tourettes and encourage him/her to express themselves freely
11 Scream, shout and chant whenever the feeling overtakes you
12 When the game finishes… go to the pub

The idea stirred a raft of responses from readers, including one who suggested we could do without the Bovril!

They were fun-filled times, but the Millennium couldn't come quick enough for me as I made plans to escape back south and to real football.

The escape took place in March 2001… but I only got as far as Tyneside.

But all things football and Brighton and Hove Albion related were only just about to kick off!

Ceefax was the world's first Teletext information service and a
forerunner to the current BBC Red Button service.
Ceefax was started by the BBC in 1974 and ended at 23:32:19
BST on 23 October 2012, in line with the digital switchover
being completed in Northern Ireland.
The very last Ceefax message read:
"By the time you read this, I will be dead.
When I started out in 1974, I was the future – TV's first robot
newsreader. But what once seemed cutting-edge is now
regarded as hopelessly old-fashioned, and I have been frozen
out by the powers that be, yet another victim of BBC ageism.
I can't take it anymore. It is a struggle to get up for the
nightshift, and my poor pixels are tired. My friend Oracle said
it would end like this.
Goodbye cruel world."

Who Ate All the Pies? Edinburgh

Scotland's capital is famous for many items of food and drink... whisky, shortbread and Edinburgh Rock all spring to mind. But unique to the city's fish and chip shops and matches at Tynecastle, Easter Road and Meadowbank is Edinburgh Chippy Sauce.

It is the local substitute for vinegar. It has to be tried to be believed, and is not sold anywhere else in Scotland. Must be eaten with the array of seafood available in Leith and washed down with Edinburgh's own Deuchars beer.

Chapter Eleven

Cider – an Albion Champagne
Edgar Street
3 May 1997

The packed Blackfriars Street stand at Edgar Street on 3rd May 1997
© Mark Raven

On 8th February 1997, fans of Arsenal, Liverpool, Spurs, Charlton Athletic, Preston North End and countless other English football clubs mingled with Real Madrid, Eintracht Frankfurt and Red Star Belgrade supporters - all in their team colours - on the crumbling terraces of the Goldstone Ground. They had travelled from across the UK and beyond to watch visitors Hartlepool United take on Brighton and Hove Albion, then rooted firmly at the very bottom of the Football League.
But more importantly, they were there to stand side-by-side with beleaguered Albion fans, as our club teetered on the very edge of extinction.

With supporters fighting a bitter war against the club's despised owners, home games in the 1996/97 season had been played in front of ever-dwindling crowds, and in an increasingly desperate and hostile atmosphere.

But this was different. Despite the cold and damp of a foggy afternoon, this felt like a carnival. The Albion players rose to the occasion, thrashing Hartlepool 5–0.

Before the game, the Albion were rooted to the bottom of League Division 3 on just 22 points, seven points adrift of Doncaster Rovers in 23rd place and eight behind Hereford United in 22nd place. We had won just five league games and lost 18.

We were poor on the pitch and in deep trouble off it.

We were at the bottom of the bottom division going into the New Year, and faced going out of the League.

Jimmy Case, whose time as manager looked so promising, lost his job after a humiliating home FA Cup replay defeat against non-league Sudbury Town, followed by another home defeat against strugglers Darlington.

Steve Gritt was appointed Albion manager in December 1996, when Albion were 11 points adrift at the foot of League Division 3, with one club to be demoted out of the League. The crowds and atmosphere at the Goldstone were at an all-time low.

And to make matters worse, just 48 hours before Gritt's appointment, the FA imposed a two-point deduction for a pitch invasion during the October match against Lincoln City as fans protested against the sale of the Goldstone by Archer and Bellotti. With just 16 games left, relegation out of the Football League – and likely extinction as a cash-strapped football club - looked an odds-on certainty.

But a miracle occurred after that Fans United Day game against Hartlepool…. suddenly the Albion went on a run to win seven and draw two of the next 14 games, including a breathtaking 1-0 victory against Doncaster Rovers in the last ever game at the Goldstone Ground on 26th April.

The huge gap between the club and Hereford United had been whittled away until the two sides ended up level on 46 points with Brighton just ahead on goal difference when the two clubs met at

Edgar Street in the final game of the 1996/97 season on 3rd May. Everything was set up perfectly to make this a match the ultimate relegation decider.

Which meant in simple terms a draw or better would see the Albion survive and Hereford go out of the league in their place.

Meanwhile I was still living in Scotland and working at *The Scotsman* in Edinburgh, some 338 miles away from Hereford. I had not done any football related reporting since my time as a weekly newspaper hack in Stranraer some three years earlier.

But having missed the 1983 Cup Final, I was determined to do everything in my power to make the 676 mile round trip, to see what might be my club's last ever game.

So on the Monday before the game (28th April) I approached my line manager and the paper's sports editor for permission to cover the match, with the twisted excuse that the chances were that an historic English football club could go out of existence the following weekend.

Neither of my bosses were interested in a straight match report, but after I explained that this was the biggest game in English football that weekend, they agreed a 1,000 word feature for the following Monday's paper would be welcome, provided I didn't make any claim for the jaunt on company expenses.

Next came the really tricky bit… getting a ticket for the game, as I certainly wouldn't be given press accreditation for a Scottish daily newspaper for a bottom tier English football game that was already sold out.

I had one idea….

I had lived in Ludlow and Herefordshire for seven years between 1982 and 1989 and knew Hereford well. I also had quite a few good friends who I had maintained contact with over the ensuing years.

My first phone call to a friend named Colin, who was on the ground staff at Edgar Street, turned up trumps.

"I can't get you into the away section," he told me, *"But if you don't wear club colours I can get a seat for you in the main stand."*

I thanked him profusely, before he added, *"It will cost you a couple of pints of cider!"*

Already I could feel my heart pounding loudly as I left work early on Friday 2nd May and drove 94 miles from Edinburgh to Corbridge to break the journey and stay with my elderly Aunt Betty for the night. She made me welcome with a huge Friday night dinner. And whether it was indigestion or just pre-match nerves, I hardly slept a wink that night. At the break of dawn the next day, under an overcast sky, I set off to drive the remaining miles along the A69, M6 and A49 to Hereford – stopping just once for a quick comfort break.

I arrived just before 1pm and found a local car park off Widemarsh Street, and walked the short distance to *The Herdsman* pub to meet Colin at our pre-arranged time and collect my solitary ticket.

The weather was typically English with bright sunny spells and downpours of rain. All around me the atmosphere was buzzing with supporters of both sides and police officers seemed to martial every turn and crossing in each road across the town.

Then spot-on 1.30pm, I looked up to see Colin's beaming face smiling at me. We shook hands before he said, in his broad Herefordshire accent: *"You must be fucking mad boy… you know you're gonna lose."*

I bought us both a pint of Bulmers cider and we sat and chatted over the lost years since we had last seen each other.

With my match ticket secured in my inside jacket pocket, Colin said he would walk with me to the main stand to ensure I got into the ground without any hassle.

As we parted, he slapped me on the back and said: *"I'll meet you back at The Herdsman after the game for a celebratory jar of cider for me and something to drown your sorrows, boy!"*

And he laughed like only Colin could.

If the atmosphere outside the ground was buzzing, inside it was electric and at times boisterous. The whole day was beginning to feel like a Cup Final.

As I made my way to my allotted seat, and remembering what had happened all those years earlier at Barnsley, I kept repeating a silent mantra: *"Don't cheer too loudly for the Albion."*

The lack of sleep from the night before was beginning to catch up with me. I found myself blinking in the rays of sun which occasionally spread across the Edgar Street turf beneath me, which looked like a gluepot after the heavy rain just an hour earlier.

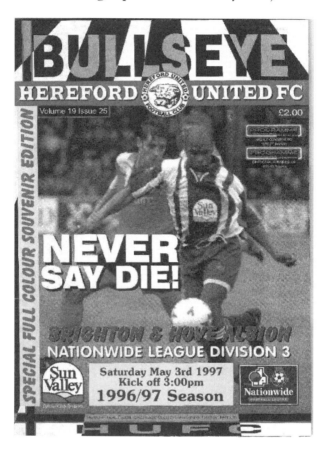

By the time of kick-off, some 3,300 Albion fans had taken over the Blackfriars Street section of the ground and were making a huge noise in a bustling crowd of 8,532.

Everyone seemed full of every emotion you could imagine: excitement, trepidation, anxiety, fear and apprehension… and even a few tears.

Our team that day was a familiar mix of youth and experience… this was the team that had battled their way from oblivion just five months earlier.

In front of keeper Mark Ormerod were John Humphrey, Stuart Tuck, Jeff Minton, Ross Johnson, Kerry Mayo, Mark Morris, Stuart Storer, Ian Baird, Craig Maskell and Paul MacDonald.

Before the game kicked off, an unbelievably calm and composed Steve Gritt was quoted as saying, *"There's an awful lot at stake here today."* Playing down the fear of thousands of football fans, the Albion manager showed everyone that he was the master of understatement.

We were all sat on a knife edge, Brighton and Hove Albion and Hereford supporters alike.

The feeling of nervousness around the ground was palpable and our own hopes of survival were dented after just 20 minutes, when Hereford forward Tony Agana's cross-shot was turned into his own net by Kerry Mayo (then only 19 years old), which, in one deflection, moved the Seagulls to the foot of League Division 3. As things stood, the Albion were relegating themselves from the Football League with no stadium and no future.

From the main stand I choked back phlegm from the cider of two hours earlier as I realised that the club I had supported since I was an 11-year-old boy was finished.

As I swilled a half time Bovril, I felt surges of anger against Hereford United, that idiot Kerry Mayo and the false hope of the early 1980s, but most of all against the arrogant David Bellotti, Greg Stanley and the crook Bill Archer. But inside me there was a feeling of sheer and utter helplessness.

I was tired and depressed and felt like this was the end.

Even the 3,300 plus Albion supporters on the terrace at the Blackfriars Street End had gone quiet with joint acceptance that this was going to be Hereford's day. They were playing better than us and the terrible muddy condition of the pitch seemed to favour them.

Maybe it was the intake of half-time beer and cider, or just a last hurrah but as the referee Neil Barry blew his whistle for the restart our travelling support shouted and chanted in one voice and at a deafening volume as the most important 45 minutes in the club's 96-year existence kicked off.

In my head I recalled at that moment a song by one of my all-time favourite bands Mott the Hoople – who just happened to come from Hereford. Their 1974 Top 20 hit single **The Golden Age of Rock n Roll** contained the immortal line: *"So if the going gets rough, Don't you blame us, You ninety-six decibel freaks."*

And that is how it sounded away to my left… we hadn't given up and our supporters were making as much noise as they could.

On the pitch, the Albion were just about managing to keep the deficit to 1-0 as our midfield seemed redundant in the Hereford mud. But miracles happen when you least expect them.

On 62 minutes, Craig Maskell controlled a hashed clearance by the Hereford defence and smashed a volley against the left goal post.

The ball cannoned back out; the Albion faithful held their collective breath as the ball rolled across the box where it was met by blond-haired substitute Robbie Reinelt (who had replaced Paul McDonald earlier in the second half) to angle a shot home.

I momentarily leapt to my feet as madness and hysteria ensued in the away section as the 96 decibel music hall limit was smashed by cheers and chanting.

From where I was seated it seemed the entire Albion crowd surged to the front to embrace our players and celebrate this single moment in our club's history.

All around me the juxtaposition of different emotions from the Hereford fans was palpable.

Groans, grunts and every profanity under the sun were being echoed around the stand and away to our right.

But there were still 28 minutes to go in the game and we had to hold on.

The Bulls went close to snatching a second goal but they could not put away their scoring chances.

I have never known time to pass so slowly as it did during the rest of that game. The home side piled on the pressure but the Albion held on and Hereford were down.

Brighton's reputation over the previous two seasons for pitch incursions led to rumours that, if Hereford were winning after 70 minutes, there would be a mass invasion. This meant there was the biggest-ever police presence at Edgar Street that day.

106

Consequently, when Neil Barry blew the final whistle, an army of riot-clad police, supported by a troop of dogs, marched on to the pitch to station themselves in two ranks along the half-way line.

Robbie Reinelt scores the equaliser   © The Argus

Their impassive expressions contrasted starkly with those etched on the faces of the Albion team and our supporters. Our players acknowledged our ecstatic fans on the Blackfriars' terraces.
Yet where I was sitting the emotions were dark and raw. Hereford fans swarmed from the Meadow End on to the pitch, but with no malign intent, just to put comforting arms around Hereford players who had slumped dejectedly to the ground.

Many years later Robbie Reinelt recalled the moments after he hit the goal which saved Brighton and Hove Albion: *"When the ball hit the post, it bounced straight out to me, and I knew what I had to do. I hit it as hard as I could with my left foot and it hit the back of the net. The fans behind that goal went ballistic.*

"The next thing I knew I was being mobbed by the team and I heard a voice in my ear say, "Robbie you just saved my life, mate." Of course, it was Kerry Mayo and I think at the time he meant it and we've become great mates ever since.

"I really felt for the Hereford lads, they'd given their all and it hadn't been good enough and they were absolutely devastated."

Police officers line the pitch at the final whistle   © Mark Raven

It was all over bar the shouting… and that went on well into the evening - an evening which for me meant all my best laid plans went west… west to a little village near the Welsh border at Hay-on-Wye. As I made my way down the steps of the main stand, the familiar smiling face of Colin greeted me. He held out his right hand and with tears streaming down his face he said quietly: *"Well done."* There was a pause as we embraced each other and I tried to imagine how he must be feeling.

Then he looked me in the eyes and added: *"There is no way I am letting you drive all the way back to Scotland after that."*

I butted in and tried to explain that I had to file a 1,000 word report for **The Scotsman** and be back for work on Monday.

"Okay, thank you so much," I answered, *"But I do have to make a couple of phone calls first."*

"Anyway boy," Colin continued, as if he hadn't heard me. *"Susie is cooking some tea and you're staying at ours tonight. Let tomorrow take care of itself."*

"Do it from ours," Colin replied. *"But first let's have a pint of cider at The Herdsman while the traffic clears."*

So in Hereford vernacular, we necked a jar of Bulmers cider each and by six o'clock, I was following Colin's green Fiat Panda the 20 miles to his home near Hay-on-Wye.

Once at his cottage I was met at the back door by his wife Susie - whom I had not seen for eight years – who greeted me like a long lost relation.

"Aww, I am so pleased for you," she said while giving me a huge hug, *"Colin will now be hell for the whole summer,"* she whispered before she turned to kiss her husband.

Behind me Colin, said: *"There's a phone in the dining room, as you need to make those calls."*

I first phoned my wife in Edinburgh to tell her of the change of plans. I then rang the sports copy desk at The Scotsman to check on what they required.

The familiar voice of Margo answered: *"Ah Nic, we've been waiting for you to ring. Kenny left a message an hour ago. We are getting the match report from PA, and as Brighton won, we only need a 400 word flavour piece from you. Can you file it tonight?"*

I quickly explained that the Albion hadn't actually won, but we weren't being relegated either, before agreeing to file my copy by 8pm.

So I sat in Colin and Susie's dining room writing a short piece for Monday morning's paper before filing word for word over the phone to a waiting Margo who was seated with her headphones and keyboard back in Edinburgh.

After a wonderful dinner of leek and potato pie – *"It's good for soaking up cider,"* said Colin – the three of us walked a hundred yards to their village pub.

"Best not let the locals know you're from Brighton," said Colin, *"They're normally a friendly lot, but you never know."*

The rest of the evening passed in a warm blur as I sampled four different ciders and talked endlessly about the years since I had moved north.

I still remember Colin's last words that evening: *"Cider can be any man's drink… a tonic to commiserate or champagne when you want to celebrate."*

This was my champagne day and my head was full of pleasant cider memories during the long drive back to Edinburgh the next day.

Despite the result at Edgar Street, Brighton's former owners went ahead with the sale of the old Goldstone Ground, leaving the club to share Gillingham's Priestfield Stadium for two seasons.

Brighton and Hove Albion ended the 1996/97 season in 22nd place in League Division 3 with 47 points, ahead of Hereford by just two goals on goal difference. Hereford were relegated. Champions were Fulham on 87 points, with Wigan as runners-up.

Hereford United never really recovered from that demotion to non-league. Despite promotion back to the Football League in 2008, they lasted only one season before relegation again. On 19th December 2014, the club was wound up in the High Court after a petition had been brought against it by HM Revenue and Customs for club debts of £1.3million.

Following the demise of United, a new 'phoenix club' was set up - Hereford FC. At the time of writing, Hereford play their football in the National League North (the sixth tier of the football pyramid).

Who Ate All the Pies? Hereford

Hereford is best known for its beef, its Bulmers and
Strongbow Cider and an array of brilliant local cheeses.
Trips to Edgar Street rarely offer a steak sandwich – more
often a burger. And if it's a cheese burger, it is topped by a
local cheese.
Bulmers have been making cider in Hereford since 1887 and
they account for 65% of all worldwide sales.

Chapter Twelve

Where are all the Coos, Daddy?
Brunton Park
21 April 2001

Brunton Park, the home of Carlisle United

A bright and sunny spring day in 2001 became one of the most poignant and memorable Albion related days I have ever experienced.

It was 21st April, just two months after I had ended my self-imposed 11-year exile in Scotland.

I had moved south into England, but only got as far as Tyneside and settled in a beautiful two bedroomed cottage in Ryton, some seven miles west of Newcastle and close to Throckley where my father was born and his father and grandfather had been coal miners.

In a strange way it was a sort of coming home, or finding my roots. I had started work as Chief Investigative Reporter on the *Newcastle Evening Chronicle* on Friday, 23rd February. By fate it was the same day the Government announced they had discovered an outbreak of Foot-and-Mouth Disease (FMD) on a pig farm at Heddon-on-the-Wall – just five miles from my new home.

A funeral pyre of dead cattle in Cumbria – a familiar sight over much of the UK during 2001.

The FMD quirk of fate would come to visit me in many ways over the ensuing six months both in my job as a journalist and personally too.

The outbreak of Foot-and-Mouth Disease in the United Kingdom caused a crisis in British agriculture and tourism.

The epizootic saw 2,026 cases of the disease in farms across most of the British countryside. Northumberland was badly hit, and neighbouring Cumbria was the worst affected area of the country, with 893 cases.

Each of those cases meant a farm having all of its livestock killed and burned. By the time the last case was confirmed at Whygill Head Farm in Appleby, Cumbria, on 30th September 2001, more than six million sheep, cattle and pigs had been slaughtered.

The first case to be discovered was at an abattoir in Essex in February 2001. Cases were then discovered in Devon, Northumberland and North Wales in the first week, and the first mass slaughter was held to try and contain the virus. But by the second week further cases were confirmed in Cornwall and Scotland.

The culling policy saw not just the animals on the affected farm killed, but also all the animals in the surrounding area. Exclusion zones made travel in some areas almost impossible and tourism nose-dived. Despite these measures the epidemic continued.

Meanwhile, I was trying to balance my new home life and keep in touch with my two young daughters Rhia and Shannon who I had reluctantly left behind following the separation from my partner in Scotland.

And from a selfish point of view I was also desperate to see my beloved Albion in action in what looked like a promotion season from League Division 3 under our charismatic new manager, Micky Adams.

So suddenly, during the Easter break I was able to marry the two together… family and football; with Foot and Mouth Disease following closely behind.

I collected my daughters for a week-long stay with me on Good Friday (13th April) and I was due to take them home to their mum on Sunday 22nd April.

Both my daughters had accompanied me to a few amateur football matches in Scotland and seemed to love the atmosphere of the games, with Shannon on one occasion running onto the pitch to offer an injured player a bag of crisps!

So, with Brighton playing a key end-of-season match at Carlisle, what better time to introduce them to real football and their dad's beloved passion.

After telephoning Brunton Park to check that the game wasn't all-ticket, on the Saturday morning I dressed my girls in warm blue clothing and drove the 54 miles along the A69 to Carlisle.

Rhia (7) and Shannon (5) sat in the back of the car giggling and excited about going to *"proper footie"* as they called it.

"Are Brighton, Hove and Albion all near each other?" enquired Shannon.

"Don't be silly Noni," replied Rhia, *"Albion is in Glasgow."*

I spent about 15 minutes trying to explain that Brighton and Hove are neighbouring places way down south in Sussex, which is in

Englandshire and where their granny and grandad live. But Albion is an ancient literary name for England.

"Then why are Albion Rovers in Scotland?" asked Rhia.

One of the last photos ever taken of my daughters with their late grandfather in 2003, both girls wearing England football shirts

More explanation followed, including the fact that there were also a Burton Albion and a West Bromwich Albion to contend with, and they were all separate clubs.

We crossed the Cumbria border and soon turned south west at the main A69 Brampton junction.

It was just nine miles to Brunton Park and Rhia suddenly shouted out: *"Oh look at all those coos!"*

I turned my head to the left to see a herd of about 100 Holstein Friesian cows being herded to a farm enclosure adjacent to a large field. Beyond the cows I could just make out huge stacks of timber beyond the enclosure.

I gulped and said cheerfully: *"Aren't the cows lovely."*

My daughters spent the rest of the journey into Carlisle chatting about the cows and the fact they had never seen so many "coos" together.

We soon passed Brunton Park and quickly found some off-street parking. There was a cool breeze despite the sunshine, so I wrapped up the girls and walked about a quarter of a mile to the ground.

Plenty of Albion supporters had travelled to the game, despite the 700 mile round trip for most of them.

I guess there were at least 1,000 of our fans out of the official attendance of 4,727 and we were all making plenty of noise.

More than once one of my daughters asked me to explain: *"What are they singing, daddy?"* And more than once I had to tell a white lie rather than repeat profanities to them.

Once in our seats in the East stand, the girls were given red and black balloons (our away colours that season) and told to make "lots of noise" by a member of our Supporters' Club.

Looking around me I could see instantly that it was going to be quite a family occasion with a lot of parents and kids present in our stand.

Brunton Park's capacity is 19,000, but even though the Petterill End terraces were being redeveloped at the time, a crowd of just shy of 5,000 made the ground seem rather empty and soulless… except for the Albion supporters who were making plenty of noise.

Half an hour before kick-off the teams were read out over the PA system.

Even though I had been watching from afar for 11 years, I knew ours was impressive: our former Dutch marine Michel Kuipers in goal with Kerry Mayo, Andy Crosby, Danny Cullip and Paul Watson in front of him, a midfield of Richard Carpenter, Steve Melton and enforcer Charlie Oatway across the centre of the park, with Paul Brooker out wide, and Gary Hart and wonder kid Bobby Zamora in attack.

We were surely far too powerful for 22nd placed Carlisle United… now where had I heard that before!?

At kick-off we were top of the table on 84 points after 41 games with Cardiff City second on 78 points having played one game more.

With fifth placed Hartlepool United on 68 points we were already guaranteed promotion, but a win at Brunton Park could see us as champions, depending on Cardiff's result away at York City – a game they were to draw 3-3.

The first half was a lot of huff and puff which was typical of much bottom tier English football. The Albion were shading the game but had few clear cut chances on goal. Zamora looked lively but it seemed he was not getting much support up top.

In our stand the chanting continued unabated when the half-time whistle blew. I explained to my daughters that we would have to be quick if they wanted crisps and a can of pop during the interval. And as soon as they had taken a toilet break and gathered refreshments we were back in our seats.

Me in the crowd at Carlisle that day: wearing specs in the centre of the photograph © BHAFC

While we were gone it seemed that a few hundred Carlisle supporters had decided to move closer to our end of the East stand and begin their own chanting. Particularly vocal were a bunch of about six clearly intoxicated Cumbrian women, who were being particularly abusive to our crowd.

My daughters were entranced by the fact that the other team's fans were also allowed to chant and sing.

Suddenly, a group of a few score Albion fans behind us retorted with a few choruses of Baha Men's recent top ten hit *"Who Let the Dogs Out?"*

Laughter erupted all around us as more Albion supporters joined in. To my right I could see Rhia and Shannon looking at each other in bemusement, before the older girl asked: *"Where are the dogs? I can't see them."*

I tried to keep from laughing too loud and placated them by saying that it was *"only a song"*.

Paul Brooker lets fly at the Carlisle goal   © **BHAFC**

The second half passed with more huff and puff football with Paul Brooker and Bobby Zamora coming close and despite three substitutions – including bringing on striker Lee Steele – the game petered out to a 0-0 draw.

118

After the final whistle Brighton had 85 points from 42 games and Cardiff City 79 points from 43 games. So we hadn't quite made it. But the Championship was all but sealed three days later when Cardiff lost 2-1 at Mansfield, and the following Saturday we went on to beat Macclesfield Town 4-1.

Meanwhile, the drive back to Ryton became sadly memorable. Nine miles out of Carlisle on the A69 we again passed the farm we had seen on the outward journey some five hours earlier.

I gulped and felt tears fill my eyes as Rhia asked: *"Where are all the coos, daddy?"*

A parent should never lie to their children, but I had told a lot of white lies that day and instinctively I answered: *"They have probably gone off for their tea."* About 100 yards beyond the farm enclosure, a plume of black smoke covered the hillside.

Despite the Government putting the blame for the 2001 Foot-and-Mouth Disease outbreak on bad practice at the Heddon-on-the-Wall pig farm, it later transpired that the British, Canadian, US and Mexican governments had been preparing for the outbreak of Foot and Mouth disease four months before it emerged on Tyneside.

An investigation I led at the *Newcastle Evening Chronicle* discovered that all four countries were staging a co-ordinated Foot and Mouth simulation exercise in October 2000, despite the fact that Britain had not been struck by the disease for 34 years and the USA and Canada had not been affected since 1929.

And Northern timber merchants also confirmed that they were approached for urgent supplies to tackle the disease by Ministry of Agriculture officials as early as December.

Scientists called for the Government to admit it knew that Foot and Mouth was present in the UK long before it was officially pinpointed at the Heddon-on-the-Wall farm on 23rd February. The Government to this day has remained very quiet and refused to respond to these claims.

Brighton and Hove Albion finished the 2000/2001 season as League Division 3 champions with 92 points, ahead of second placed Cardiff City on 82 points.

Who Ate All the Pies? Carlisle

Like most English football grounds, pies, hot dogs and burgers are fans' favourites. But Carlisle United has one item of food not found at any other Football League ground (now Workington Town are languishing in the Northern Premier League) and that is a Cumberland Sausage Ring served in a bun with either red or brown sauce. It is enough to keep you full for a whole 90 minutes!

Chapter Thirteen

Death in Grimsby
Blundell Park
14 February 2004

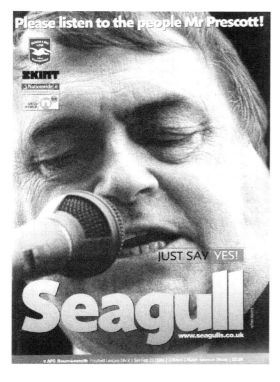

The lobbying of John Prescott to grant planning permission for Falmer was persistent

We are all going to die one day, but I never thought that my day would be on a cold and wet Saturday afternoon in Grimsby, a day pervaded by the smell of rotting fish entrails and unrelenting rain.

Yet the day all started out so brightly and so well planned.

By the start of 2004, the campaign for a new stadium had been in full swing for four years, yet we seemed no nearer to achieving the dream of a new stadium at Falmer than we were at the time of the Millennium.

Terrace chants, postcards to local MPs, flags, badges, Tshirts and banners and even the pouring of buckets of water over celebrities were all part of the movement to heighten awareness of our club's desperate need for a new stadium.

The pressure was building on Deputy Prime Minister John Prescott, who held the government's planning portfolio and the ultimate rubber stamp, to agree to the proposal for Falmer.

The project had been the subject of a public inquiry, with Mr Prescott having the final say on its outcome. So what better way to show we were on his side than to hand the main man a Valentine's Card at his constituency office in Kingston-upon-Hull.

But this wasn't any old Valentine's card… it was huge and under the heading *"Be Our Valentine Mr Prescott,"* was the poem: *"Roses are red, Brighton are blue, Our club's future is all down to you. Please say YES to our new stadium."*

And by chance Valentine's Day 2004 fell on a Saturday and by a bigger irony, the Albion were set to play a regulation away league fixture against Grimsby Town just 35 miles south of the Humber at Blundell Park.

But the final irony was a personal one… I had been born in Hull. We moved south to Sussex when I was just three years old and in the ensuing 44 years, I had never been back to the place of my birth. So the Valentine's Day of action was formalised.

As many Albion fans as possible were asked to turn up at 11am on Saturday 14th February outside the Hull East MP's office where the giant card would be handed directly to Mr Prescott.

So early on Saturday I set off in my new company car to drive the 144 miles from my home on Tyneside down the A1 and M62 to Hull.

I ensured I was wearing my short-sleeved centenary Albion shirt, scarf and a lightweight shower-proof blue jacket as I left South Shields at about 7.30am in bright but breezy conditions.

The journey was also a breeze but as I approached Hull around 10.30am, I noticed some specks of rain.

I muttered a quiet *"Oh shit"* to myself as I realised I had forgotten to bring neither a brolly nor a waterproof coat with me. But at the

Albion fans hand over the giant Valentine card to John Prescott's East Hull constituency office where it is received by his agent

time, I thought little more of it than just an annoyance. It was to be an annoyance which nearly cost me my life later that day.

I arrived outside John Prescott's constituency office just in time and parked in a side road opposite. Over the road I noticed a coach was parked and a clutch of between 30 and 50 fans in the familiar blue and white stripes were gathered together.

The weather was certainly a lot cooler than it was on Tyneside, as I remembered my mum's words: *"Hull was the coldest place we ever lived… we couldn't wait to move away."*

So I joined the group of fellow Brighton fans as the giant card was handed formally to Mr Prescott's agent Harry Woodford – the great man himself had other business that day.

123

We all exchanged a few pleasantries and posed for photographs before we set off in cars and the coach across the Humber Bridge to the game against Grimsby.

In same way that Crystal Palace play at Croydon and Arsenal don't play at Greenwich, Grimsby Town's ground isn't in Grimsby, but three miles south at Cleethorpes – a sort of northern Bognor Regis, but with more pot holes and boarded up shops.

Looking back, I now see that a year earlier (2003) Hull had been voted number 1 in a best-selling guide to the UK's crap towns and Cleethorpes is often referred to as the *"Last Resort"*.

Grimsby Town's Blundell Park

As I arrived in the town, with rain lashing down and taking care to avoid a missing man-hole cover in the road, I drove directly to Blundell Park to look for a car park. There was not one to be found. So I stopped to ask a friendly policeman where it was safe to park. He explained that there was no free parking near the ground and suggested I find some off-street parking to the west of the A180. So after a bit of driving around, at about 1.30pm I eventually found a small side street about a mile from Blundell Park and parked my car safely outside a smart looking terraced house. By now the rain was lashing down and a strong wind blowing off the North Sea. As I began to walk to the ground I realised the enormous mistake of not bringing warmer clothes or a waterproof coat.

And as I stood at the away supporters' turnstile I was soaked to the skin and began shivering.

Once inside I immediately looked for the catering caravan and ordered a hot Bovril and a meat pie.

This would surely sustain me.

The weather was really foul and before kick-off I had consumed a second Bovril and was unsure which of my body parts or limbs were wetter or colder than the others.

The attendance was a meagre 3,673 in this League Division 2 fixture and the final irony of the day was not lost on anyone that both our clubs had been relegated from League Division 1 together following a tame 2-2 draw at the same stadium in front of double the number of fans the previous May.

Now everything about this fixture looked depressing from our third choice goalkeeper Stuart Jones, through our ageing centre backs Cullip and Butters to our lightweight forwards of Jake Robinson and Leon Knight.

But the most depressing was the state of the pitch, which after 30 minutes of play was a quagmire with the goalmouths in particular becoming mud baths.

From kick-off it seemed that Robinson and Knight had problems moving or passing in the mud.

Grimsby scored inside five minutes through Isaiah Rankin and a mistake by keeper Jones.

Trevor Benjamin equalised on 18 minutes. But in the mud and the rain it was hardly a football match and seemed we were going to be lucky to snatch even a point. And so it was at 75 minutes, when substitute Phil Jevons seemed to bundle Stuart Jones over as he scrambled the ball into the net.

Danny Cullip remonstrated with the referee Roy Pearson that our keeper had been fouled, but the goal stood.

Grimsby were playing dirty in the mud and picked up four bookings before Aidan Davies was given a straight red and sent off in the 90th minute.

We still lost 2-1 in one of the direst games I have ever witnessed between two equally dire sides.

Richard 'Chippy' Carpenter breaks from midfield in the lashing rain at Blundell Park © BHAFC

At the time it didn't really matter to me, because after numerous cups of hot drinks and at least three hot pies, all I wanted to do was get back to my car and try to refind some blood circulation and warmth.

So I walked quickly back to where I had parked my car with my jeans soaked to my legs and my trainers squelching under my feet. I started the car's engine and turned the heating control to full and hoped that by revving the engine some warm air might circulate.

But while my bottom felt like I was sitting in a pool of melting ice cream, my whole body started to shiver vigorously. So I took off my wet Albion scarf and wrapped it around my belly in a vain effort to keep warm.

It was then I noticed how yellowy white my fingers were on the steering wheel and how numb my feet and hands had become. I was shivering all over.

I telephoned my wife on my old Nokia mobile to tell her I would be late home and mentioned how cold I was. She suggested that only by running the car properly would the engine heat up and allow the heating system to work.

By now it was 5.20pm and getting dark as I made to move the automatic gear into Drive and carefully pulled away from the kerb. But I could not seem to co-ordinate my feet on the accelerator and brake, so even for an automatic car, my pulling away was jumpy. Also my vision appeared odd, although at the time I thought it was just the amount of rain on the screen that was obscuring my sight of the road.

I slowly drove the car down the side street and turned north on the A180 towards Grimsby and the road home.

Suddenly a loud horn sounded behind me and a driver was flashing his headlights. In an instant, I realised I had forgotten to turn on my own car lights.

I was shivering violently and start to convulse as I drove slowly along the main road.

The rest I don't remember very well.

But by the time I was alongside Grimsby dock I had managed to stall my car… quite how anyone can stall an automatic vehicle is still beyond belief.

I think at this point I must have blacked out.

Suddenly a pedestrian was banging on my passenger side window and mouthing something at me. The rest was a blur.

I later discovered that this pedestrian, called Kevin, had immediately recognised something was wrong with me and called an ambulance and the police.

When I woke in a bed in the A&E department of the Diana, Princess of Wales Hospital in Grimsby I was wrapped in what appeared to be a silver space blanket, had a drip in my left arm and a young nurse was rubbing my right hand.

A view of Grimsby Dock Tower close to where my car stalled and I blacked out
© Nigel Hardy

I was given a hot cup of tea and some medication before I noticed that all my clothes were missing and I was wearing what appeared to be hospital pyjamas.

"Don't worry," said the nurse, a young woman in her mid-20s called Samantha, *"We are drying your clothes for you… you have hypothermia."*
Later that evening I was moved to intensive care and monitored every 20 minutes throughout the night.

The next morning a polite doctor told me that my core temperature when the ambulance had arrived the previous evening was 35.2 degrees.

"Much lower or much longer, that would have been your last football match," he said with a smile.

"This isn't sunny Brighton you know," he added, with a touch of irony.

Brighton and Hove Albion finished the 2003/04 season in 4th place in League Division 2 with 77 points. Champions were Plymouth Argyle on 90 points. We were to win the Play-off Final 1-0 against Bristol City at the Millennium Stadium in Cardiff – after beating Swindon Town in the semi-final - with the only goal a penalty by Leon Knight, and secure promotion back to League Division 1.

Poor Grimsby finished in 21st place with 50 points and faced back-to-back relegation.

Who Ate All the Pies? Grimsby

Grimsby is England's biggest fishing port and also boasts having the freshest fish and the best fish and chips in the entire UK.

I may have survived that day in 2004 on a diet of Bovril, meat pies and luck, but any trip to Blundell Park has to be accompanied by Fish and Chips.

Chapter Fourteen

Why are we in Bloody Berwick?
Shielfield Park
6 March 2004

My eldest son Ben and I handing out *Falmer For All* petitions and information leaflets outside Shielfield Park, Berwick-Upon-Tweed

When you're down at the bottom, the only way is up. And for Brighton and Hove Albion, our club had been down at the bottom since about 1995.
Like most football clubs, Brighton and Hove Albion has had its share of heroes and villains. But the real villains in the history of our

club number just three: former owners Bill Archer and Greg Stanley along with chief executive David Bellotti.

In the mid-1990s, it slowly became clear to us that this trio planned to sell off our beloved Goldstone Ground to property developers – who wanted to place a retail park on the site – and to move our club to a shiny new stadium.

We initially welcomed the idea as we were assured nothing would be done until a suitable new home was found.

But in 1995, *The Argus* (our local daily newspaper) revealed that Bellotti, Archer and Stanley had agreed a deal with developers Chartwell Land, without any provisions for the future.

The true motives behind the deal became evident when it was then revealed that Archer had altered the club's constitution to allow directors to profit from the sale of the ground.

Fans were now faced with the harsh reality that the trio's interest in the Albion's future went little further than topping up their own bank balances, and that they had washed their hands of the club's future.

The 1996/97 season became one of football's great displays of non-violent direct action, as we staged a desperate rebellion against this trio and saved our club in the process.

Albion fans organised protests in the city centre, pitch invasions and walk-outs at the Goldstone Ground and even lobbied outside Archer's business headquarters in Crewe – some 230 miles away. Former Lib-Dem MP Bellotti – who still attended matches – was overwhelmed with abuse and forced to flee the stadium on several occasions.

That season also included the first Fans United Day, when on 8th February 1997, supporters of clubs across the UK and Europe – many wearing their own club colours - shared the Goldstone terraces in solidarity with the Albion fans. Throughout the season visiting fans had often shown support of the Albion's plight with banners and placards, but not before to this extent.

And it was the kick-start we fans needed, for from that day onwards we all knew we were not alone.

The Albion fans fought hard and eventually succeeded in wrestling the club away from the asset stripping owners. Sadly the victory had all come too late to save the Goldstone Ground and the next battle commenced to find a new home. That search took up much of the next decade.

In the week before the last Goldstone game an agreement was reached between local advertising executive and entrepreneur Dick Knight and Bill Archer for control of the club, thanks to professional mediators brought in by the Football Association. Dick and his colleagues had taken their seats in the directors' box for the match, but in fact the deal wasn't legally enacted until September 1997.

By then the Goldstone Ground had been demolished, and Albion had survived a vote to expel them from the Football League.

Now the team, which had secured survival against Hereford in May that year, was playing its "home" games 75 miles away at Gillingham's Priestfield Stadium where the crowds were pitifully small, averaging just 2,300 in 1997/98. The performances were terrible, far worse than in 1996/97, and only three "home" games were won; but Doncaster Rovers were even worse and occupied the one relegation place to preserve the Albion's Football League status once more.

The 1998/99 season was better, but the priority was to get the club back to Brighton or Hove if it were to survive.

A fans' campaign to *"Bring Home the Albion"* supported an application to use Withdean Stadium – primarily an athletics track – as a temporary home pending the construction of a new stadium in the Brighton area.

The campaign succeeded, despite some local opposition, and Brighton and Hove Albion moved into Withdean in 1999, thrashing Mansfield Town 6-0 in the first league game there.

But Withdean had severe limitations. There was only one small roof to keep spectators dry, so most fans sat in temporary stands beyond the running track, exposed to the elements.

The initial capacity was just 6,000, but additional seating was provided over the years and by 2008 it reached the heady heights of 8,800.

It was never a proper football ground, but Withdean kept the club alive for 12 years – just as Gillingham had for two years – and it proved to be a pretty successful venue for the Albion with back to back Champions in 2000/01 and 2001/02, play-off promotion in 2003/04 and a final promotion to the Championship in 2010/11. Our years at Withdean provided a quirky irony for me for on 16th July 1966, as a 10-year-old Wolf Cub I had attended a national Jamboree at the same stadium in front of Lady Baden Powell on a gloriously hot summer's day.

My abiding memory of that day is the PA announcement during the Jamboree that Bobby Charlton had just scored a 25 yard goal against Mexico in the World Cup – a game England went on to win 2-0. Little did I know back then that my club would end up playing its own football on those same fields north of Preston Park.

While Withdean provided breathing space for the Albion in the new Millennium, all efforts were concentrated on a site on the edge of Brighton at Falmer that the club – and the local council – had identified as the best for a new stadium, given its ready access to public transport and its partly-developed nature.

Masterminded by chief executive Martin Perry, the plans would give the club a bright future, but first, permission had to be secured from the city council and then, because of the sensitive nature of the site, from the government.

Once again, our supporters undertook a lengthy campaign to back the plans and win over the politicians. In May 1999, they secured a 68% vote in favour (at a local referendum) and followed it with a 61,000 signature petition and some intense lobbying.

The opposition was also determined though, and a public inquiry lasting many months was held, but the results were inconclusive. However, a second inquiry concluded that Falmer – just north of Brighton - was the only viable location for a stadium in the area, and the Government decided that the development was in the public interest because of its social and economic benefits for the more deprived areas of Brighton.

But it almost didn't happen.

Because of the cost of the public enquiry into planning permission for a new stadium, rent on Withdean Stadium, fees paid to use Gillingham's Priestfield Stadium, and a general running deficit due to the low ticket sales inherent in a small ground, the club had an accumulated deficit of £9.5 million in 2004.

Lobbying for Falmer at the Millennium Bridge in Gateshead

The board of directors paid £7 million of this; the other £2.5 million had to be raised from the operations of the club. In an effort to achieve this, a fund-raising appeal known as the *Alive and Kicking Fund* was started, with everything from nude Christmas Cards featuring the players, picture postcards of Scenes Around Brighton and Hove to send to every MP in the country, to a CD single being released to raise cash.

The CD *We Want Falmer* by an ad-hoc band named Seagulls Ska, and fronted by long time Albion activist Attila the Stockbroker (aka John Baine), was a particular success. As a pastiche on the original Piranah's hit *Tom Hark* it reached number 17 in the charts and stayed in the Top 40 for three weeks. It also became the Albion anthem on the terraces for the next three seasons.

Running alongside this was a publicity campaign nicknamed *Falmer For All* to raise awareness of:
* Brighton and Hove Albion's homeless plight
* The need for the new stadium at Falmer
* The need for political support for the planning application.
Part of this campaign was *National Falmer Day* on Saturday 6th March 2004… less than a month after my near death experience in Grimsby.
The day was chosen because our scheduled league game with Tranmere Rovers had been postponed due to their progress in the FA Cup, leaving us all with a football free weekend – at least on the South Coast.
So all Albion fans were encouraged to travel to other matches to help publicise our campaigns. Organisers also arranged for a publicity piece to be placed in the programmes of each club to be visited.

The schedule that day reads like a **Who's Who** of League and Non-League English football:

Manchester United v Fulham
Crystal Palace v Reading
Gillingham v Nottingham Forest
Norwich City v Ipswich Town
Rotherham United v Bradford City
West Ham v Walsall
Bournemouth v Wycombe Wanderers
Colchester United v Hartlepool
QPR v Oldham Athletic
Rushden and Diamonds v Peterborough United
Swindon Town v Brentford
Wrexham v Grimsby Town
Boston United v Rochdale
Bury v Leyton Orient
Cambridge United v Northampton Town
Cheltenham Town v Lincoln City
Oxford United v Huddersfield Town
Swansea City v Doncaster Rovers
Torquay United v Carlisle United
Stevenage Borough v Woking
Crawley Town v Weymouth Town
Eastbourne Borough v Hednesford Town
Bognor Regis Town v Kingstonian
Corinthian Casuals v Lewes
AFC Wimbledon v Cobham

Due to the fact that I was living on Tyneside and neither Newcastle United nor Sunderland had a home game that weekend, I volunteered for the most northerly fixture on **National Falmer Day:** a Scottish Second Division game between Berwick Rangers v Hamilton Academicals and Shielfield Park – average attendance 521. Although Berwick is definitely in England (more than two miles south of the Scottish Border), its football club is deemed Scottish. Formed in 1881, Berwick Rangers affiliated to the Scottish Football Association around 1905 and entered the Scottish Border League in the same year.

So my job that day was to try and persuade about 500 Scottish football fans to support the plight of an English club some 410 miles away. It seemed like a lost cause.

But sometimes football really surprises you!

Postcards from the edge of survival

And Saturday 6th March 2004 is a day that will stay with me for many years to come.

It all began at my home in South Shields as my wife, sister-in-law and I decked out two cars in blue and white and A4 Falmer posters on a warm and sunny morning.

We bundled my eldest son Ben (then 19) and my youngest Nathan (just two years old) into the first car and, in convoy, we made a pleasant and fairly speedy journey up the north east coast – via the A1 - to beautiful Berwick-upon-Tweed.

Shielfield Park is a particularly quaint ground and only spoilt by a speedway track running between the terraces and seated stands and the pitch. It had a certain feel of Withdean about it.

Arriving at 1pm we were immediately welcomed at the gates by the club secretary Denis McCleary and Berwick Rangers chairman Robert Wilson.

After friendly handshakes we were shown inside the ground and offices and sincerely informed that they were all 100% behind the *Falmer for All* campaign. Berwick had suffered similar ground problems to our own some years earlier and clearly these things live long in people's memories.

We were then invited to go to the club bar where we would be made welcome. We took their generous advice and enjoyed a couple of pints and half an hour of good chat with 40 or so Berwick and Hamilton club members who were finishing their lunch and having a wee bevvy (Scottish slang for a drink)

We handed out our *National Falmer Day* leaflets while many fellow football fans signed pre-printed letters to John Prescott and we took other names and postcodes for our petition.

Outside the bar we bought a match day programme with a fabulous half-page piece inside about our need for Falmer.

As fans of both clubs started arriving for the game many mentioned that they had already read of our plight in the local newspaper the *Berwick Advertiser,* the previous day.

We then set about leafleting and lobbying every fan, coach driver, police officer, player or club official we could find.

By 3pm all of our leaflets were gone.

Everyone, without exception was supportive and I was surprised how many knew the ins and outs of our history – some even mentioned the names Bellotti and Archer as "scum".

I found that amazing, given the distance and the fact that our clubs play in different countries.

A good few also chatted about how Brighton was an old established "big club" and how it would be a travesty if we failed. Even the Hamilton supporters who came from near Glasgow were supportive and wanted to hear of sunny Brighton!

So by 3pm we went into the ground warmed and in good spirit. Initially we had decided to support each side for 15 minutes in turn. But given the welcome by Berwick – and the fact they are English – we stood with the Berwick crowd and joined them for a mutton pie and Bovril at half time.

For Nathan, it was an extra special day as it was his first ever football match.

In between eating crisps and sweets he had the Berwick crowd roaring... whenever he saw a seagull (there were loads) he would shout *"Seagulls"*.

Ben, my wife and I tried a chorus of *"Stand up if you want Falmer"*, but as only five joined in, we thought quiet discretion was a better ploy!

As for the football... it was forgettable kick and rush rubbish. A 4-2 defeat for Berwick and not one of the goals was memorable – in fact I missed one as I turned around to stop Nathan from pinching a guy's Bovril.

But as for the day itself I will never forget it.

And more importantly it was a small part of our **National Falmer Day** event. I counted and we handed out 420 leaflets (pretty much the entire crowd!) and letters. We also had about 20 letters signed and handed back immediately.

Reading through some of them later that evening I was amazed to find that two were signed by guys from Doncaster, one from Sheffield and another from Liverpool! **National Falmer Day** really was a national event.

On 28th October 2005 the Office of the Deputy Prime Minister announced that the application for Falmer had been successful, to the joy of every Albion fan.

But Lewes District Council contested John Prescott's decision to approve the planning permission, forcing a judicial review. This was based on a minor error in Prescott's original approval which neglected to state that some car parking for the stadium is in the Lewes district as opposed to the Brighton and Hove unitary authority. This caused further delay.

But the dream of a new community stadium had been achieved. But more patience was needed to build the dream… our new Field of Dreams.

Once the judicial review ruled in favour of the stadium, Lewes District Council said that it would not launch any further appeals

But it delayed the final permission until 2007 – 10 ten years after the site was first identified.

Then came the task of funding the construction. Tony Bloom, local millionaire and a long-term supporter of the club, stepped up to take over from Dick Knight and provide around £100 million for the new stadium and then another £30 million for a new training complex at Lancing.

The Amex Community Stadium was finally opened seven years later in July 2011.

Who Ate All the Pies? Berwick

There are two foodstuffs associated with all Scottish football
grounds. One is the Forfar Bridie, a peppery puff pastry fold of
minced meat, and the other is Mutton Pie – often called a
Scotch Pie. It is the latter which is a real fans' favourite
whether you are at Ibrox, Park Head or Shielfield Park.
Minced/diced mutton or lamb in a boiled pastry case. Quite
simply, attending any Scottish football match is not the same
without one!

Chapter Fifteen

Stopping the Wrecking Ball
The Racecourse
20 November 2004

Fans United at The Racecourse – I am pictured far right

Since my first game in 1967, I have witnessed many highs and lows following my beloved Brighton and Hove Albion.
And the 1996/97 season became one of football's great displays of non-violent direct action, as we staged a desperate fight against three asset strippers (Bill Archer, Greg Stanley and David Bellotti) who were stealing our club from under our noses.
That season included the first Fans United Day, when on 8th February 1997, supporters of clubs across the UK and Europe shared the Goldstone terraces in solidarity with the Albion fans. We eventually succeeded in our battle to save our club. But the victory came too late to save the Goldstone Ground.

143

Over the ensuing years the story of asset-stripping football club owners was replicated far too many times for comfort.

By the time I became involved in a similar battle, seven years had passed. I was living 300 miles away on Tyneside and by a quirk of fate was unexpectedly thrust the mantle of Fans United organiser for Wrexham FC, a club nestling just a few miles on the Welsh side of the English border.

Their supporters were battling their owner Alex Hamilton and his chairman Mark Guterman, who had threatened to bulldoze their ground for a housing development.

But they were facing an uphill battle for anyone outside North Wales to recognize their plight.

Brighton and Hove Albion fans had all been alerted to their battle during our last League One game on 8th May 2004 at the Racecourse, a game we won 2-0.

But my own involvement started with a random trip of five fellow Brighton supporters to the old Belle Vue Stadium in Doncaster on 2nd October that year for a regulation League One match against Wrexham to show our support for their battle for survival.

The bitter irony was that during our own battle against Bellotti, Archer and Stanley in 1997, Doncaster Rovers had endured a similar plight against their rogue owner, Ken Richardson.

A fire in the Belle Vue main stand in June 1995 caused extensive damage. Nine months later Richardson was arrested charged with conspiracy to commit arson as part of an insurance fraud and was subsequently found guilty. He was sentenced to four years imprisonment. The actual arsonist, 41-year-old Tyneside man Alan Kristiansen, received a one-year prison sentence; it was revealed that Kristiansen had been paid £10,000 by Richardson to start the fire.

And through friendship and solidarity in adversity, Doncaster and Albion fans had developed a strong bond.

Anyway, fast forward to 2004!

Once a journalist, always a journalist, and in the week before the game at Belle Vue I had alerted the local press about our intention to attend the game and I detailed the reasons for the visit.

So on a sunny autumn Saturday a new three way bond was formed between the fans of three diverse Football League clubs.

144

Brighton and Hove Albion, Doncaster Rovers and Wrexham Fans United at the old Belle Vue Stadium

Armed with placards and wearing our distinctive blue and white stripes we made our way into the away enclosure at Doncaster Rovers with the Wrexham fans.

Along the way we had a little explaining to do with the match stewards to persuade them that we were not there to cause trouble, but to offer support to a club in crisis.

Once inside the ground Wrexham supporters began introducing themselves and asked curiously why we had come. Over the next 45 minutes there ensued a lot more banter about our respective clubs' travails and the exchange of some club lapel badges and other small mementoes.

We were all in good fraternal spirits and new friendships were born. But nothing prepared us for the PA announcement a few minutes before kick-off, when our group of six were invited onto the pitch with representatives from Wrexham and Doncaster Rovers supporters clubs to a standing ovation and chants from all around the ground of *"We Love You Brighton."*

The chanting and applause went on for what seemed like forever and I noticed my Albion friend Ade next to me shivering with emotion.

"Hey Nic," he said. *"This is fucking amazing, mate."*

The impact of our visit was tangible and unforgettable.

Such was the occasion I cannot even remember the score, though something tells me it was a 0-0 draw.

Following the game and the drive home, Ade suggested we ring BBC Radio Five's 606 football show and tell them about the afternoon.

After a bit of haggling, he suggested I make the call.

My random phone call from a layby on the A1 was greeted with similar enthusiasm by the BBC researcher and five minutes later by the show's host Alan Green.

I tried to explain everything in detail, including the history of Brighton and Hove Albion and Doncaster Rovers and more importantly, the current plight of Wrexham.

Alan Green was truly gobsmacked at the other end of the line, as he had no idea about the situation at Wrexham.

Suddenly the ball had begun rolling and more calls to the show from other football fans followed.

It almost seemed unreal, but I guess with 20 years of PR and newspaper experience and family connections to North Wales, I had found a strange and unexpected sudden niche in my life.

But what happened next was like a crazy PR rollercoaster.

Weeks of phone calls, radio and TV interviews and bombarding other football clubs' message boards (this was before the days of Facebook and Twitter) arrived… all emanating and ending at my little office above a terrace in South Shields.

And the response from friends in Brighton and our allies in Wrexham and Doncaster was that we needed another Fans United Day. This time it would be held at the Racecourse ground.

So it came to pass that Saturday 20th November 2004 is a football day I will never forget.

More than 1,500 supporters of other clubs descended on Wrexham's Racecourse Ground that afternoon for a routine third tier match against Bristol City.

The weather was wintry and cold, but that did not dampen the shared spirit.

As part of a small group of Brighton fans, I entered the famous old ground and made my way to seats on the left side of the home Mold Road stand. We were armed with a huge *"Fans United Say Save AFC Wrexham"* banner, which we were invited to place along the pitch side hoardings.

Wrexham's average home gate had been 4,500 and even at 2.45pm it was clear that there were many more than the average.

Everywhere we looked fans were filling the seats – even the terraces at Wrexham's Kop seemed full with banners and flags everywhere being waved madly by fans.

The referee even delayed kick-off by 15 minutes to allow all the fans to enter the ground safely.

Our own small group was soon augmented by more friends. We stood 16 strong and knew other Brighton supporters were elsewhere in the ground.

A bunch of Seagulls in the Mold Road Stand – far right: my good friend Ian Hine and I applaud the Wrexham supporters

Around us we met fans from Sunderland, Cardiff City and Swansea, Stoke City, Stockport County, Northampton, Everton, Wolves,

Telford, Bury, Doncaster Rovers and even Chester City (Wrexham's bitter rivals from 10 miles up the road).

As a group of us made our way to queue at the refreshment area, two Wrexham fans suddenly thrust £10 notes into our hands, with the same welcome: *"We have been instructed to buy all your guys cheeseburgers and a pint."* We each tried to refuse their generosity, but they were insistent and one guy said: *"We'd be dead if it wasn't for you."*

Back in our seats and munching happily on our burgers a chorus of *"We love you Brighton"* suddenly echoed from our left. A group of Wrexham fans were looking in our direction, singing and smiling broadly.

We replied with chants of *"Seagulls, seagulls,"* and a warm chill ran down my spine. I looked around as thousands of people rose to their feet and applauded. More choruses of *"We love you Brighton"* rang from all sides of the ground.

I glanced at my good friend Ian. *"Glad you're here?"* I asked.

"Too right, I wouldn't have missed this for anything," he replied.

The ground was full as the first half passed in repeated choruses of mutual singing and chanting.

Then a few minutes before half-time, a senior steward walked across to where we were sitting and told us: *"You can carry your banner around the pitch at half-time."*

Dazed by the offer, a handful of us followed the steward down the steps as people stood and began applauding.

If what happened at Doncaster seven weeks earlier seemed unreal, this was another galaxy.

Around the pitch side we continued following the steward. The first half was still in progress, but as we walked, each section of the ground rose to their feet and cheered and clapped – it was as if what was happening on the pitch was inconsequential.

Our collective hands were freezing but the adrenalin was rushing as we began a procession along the touchline – our *Save AFC Wrexham* banner held aloft to the crowd. Spontaneous *"We love you Brighton"* echoed again in our ears. Fans leant over the hoardings to shake our hands.

As we reached the Kop there were gathered on the pitch about 200 Wrexham fans holding their own *Save the Racecourse* banner. We walked past, shook hands, embraced and shared smiles that will last many lifetimes.

Then as we passed the player's tunnel the Wrexham club captain Brian Carey smiled and winked at us and then held out his hand. We all shook his outstretched hand as he simply said: *"Thanks so much"*.

Parading the Save AFC Wrexham banner around the Racecourse

I moved across to Ian and said: *"This surpasses anything I have ever been to in football... only the last game at the Goldstone comes close"*.

Ian smiled broadly. *"It is simply amazing"* he replied.

We made our way back to our seats, shaking more hands along the way.

But as we approached the entrance at the end of the main stand, a hefty and serious looking man in a red Wales shirt stood in our way. He looked menacing. I looked at him closely and there were tears in his eyes.

"I just want to say thank you," he said.

He thrust his giant hand into mine and shook firmly, and proceeded to ensure he shook all our hands.

On the way back to the seats we stopped to ask a steward about the attendance. She replied: *"At least 10,000!"*

Wrexham lost the game 3-1, but that did not seem to matter to anyone. Sometimes the bigger picture is more important. Wrexham faced the real prospect of liquidation after it went into administration in December 2004, just a fortnight after the Fans United day. It thankfully escaped.

Yes, that's me tackling an effigy of the loathed Wrexham chairman Mark Guterman on the Fans United Day with his bag of swag

Wrexham eventually won its battle, but not before the club was relegated from the Football League.

But over the ensuing 15 years, clubs the length and breadth of the UK have faced a similar plight. Experts estimate that since 2001, more than 40 of the 72 Football League clubs outside the

Premiership have either gone into administration or to the brink of it. In many cases the crises were the direct result of mismanagement or profiteering by club owners.

And it is not a problem confined to smaller clubs.

A few years ago Manchester City, Sheffield Wednesday and Leeds United also faced financial ruin under successive poor stewardship and questionable investment.

As I make the finishing touches to this book in the spring of 2019, Blackpool FC were given a reprieve from a 12 point deduction after going into administration following a five-year battle between its fans and the club's rogue owners.

Championship club Birmingham City decided at the same time not to appeal against a nine-point deduction it received earlier for breaching profitability and sustainability rules. League One club Coventry City still face expulsion from the League if it fails to provide a solution about where it will play home games next season. Bury FC had a winding-up petition adjourned until later in May 2019 with players and staff still to be paid their March wages. The situation there has been described as *"extremely concerning."*

And EFL chief executive Shaun Harvey offered to meet with Bolton Wanderers Supporters' Trust as the beleaguered Championship side's continued their search for a new owner after players went on strike over non-payment of their wages.

As I write this in the early Spring of 2019, Wrexham FC are still languishing in their 12th season of non-league football, but the club is now owned by the fans as a community venture and never again will they be victim to a rogue or greedy asset stripper.

But it wasn't the end of the mutual love affair between our two clubs, as I will explain later in this book.

Who Ate All the Pies? Wrexham

It ought to be something very Welsh like Bara Brith or Welsh cakes for Wrexham, or even roast lamb butties.
But to mark the occasion, here is a sample of the cheese steak burgers bought for us Albion fans by Wrexham supporters that day in November 2004.
Thank you!

Chapter Sixteen

The Prosser Principle
Deepdale
5 April 2005

The face of England legend Tom Finney graces the outside of Deepdale's main stand

There can't be many English football league referees more reviled by Brighton and Hove Albion supporters than former RAF sergeant Phil Prosser.
And we are not alone. He is similarly hated by fans of Burnley, Wigan, Walsall, Derby County and even Crystal Palace for his card happy style and habit of making bizarre game changing decisions. Thankfully, Gloucestershire born Mr Prosser, 55, is now retired from the Football League list.
But he was still very much active in 2005, and in 2002 for that matter!
"When things aren't going your way, there are times when you feel like the world is against you." is how the Brighton and Hove Albion's match day

programme described the Seagulls' 4-2 home defeat to Sheffield United in October 2002.

Except the world wasn't against the Albion – only one man was. Phil Prosser, a referee who delivered a performance so biased that he received a standing ovation from Blades' fans as he left the pitch and had a Member of Parliament from the Albion side saying he should be banned from officiating.

"The referee, in my view, gave a totally inept – some would say corrupt performance. He showed inconsistencies and bias towards Sheffield United," said Hove MP Ivor Caplin, before going on to call for the FA to launch an inquiry and to suspend Prosser while the inquiry was ongoing. The Labour MP wasn't the only Albion fan incensed by the decisions from the man in the middle. Several hundred supporters gathered on the running track at Withdean, in front of the South Stand, as the game came to its conclusion to voice their displeasure and objects were even thrown towards the pitch.

Neil Warnock's Sheffield United might have been the side in the hunt for promotion, but in the first half that day there was only one team in it as the Albion defied the form guide, which showed 10 consecutive defeats, to go into the break 2-0 ahead.

The Albion also had two strong penalty appeals turned down by Prosser, which drew plenty of anger from the Withdean faithful. Those non-awards proved costly once Warnock introduced Carl Asaba into proceedings just before the hour mark.

The Albion managed to get through the next 10 minutes unscathed until Michael Brown fired a low shot past Michel Kuipers from the edge of the box to halve the deficit. Asaba then levelled things up with 13 minutes to left to play.

It stayed 2-2 until the 86th minute when the Prosser Show began in earnest as the referee awarded two inexplicable penalties to gift Sheffield United victory.

Neither appeared a penalty to anyone else in the ground that day… neither a supposed foul by Albion keeper Michel Kuipers, nor one two minutes later when Adam Virgo was adjudged to have brushed against Wayne Allison. The decision was made all the stranger by the fact that not one visiting player appealed for a foul.

That man: card happy Phil Prosser

They didn't think it was a penalty, the Albion players didn't think it was a penalty, neither bench thought it was a penalty and nobody in the stands thought it was a penalty. Only one man thought it was! The Albion went from 2-0 up with 20 minutes to go to 4-2 down at the final whistle – all because of referee Phil Prosser.

To make matters worse, Prosser then reported that he and the Blades' striker Peter Ndlovu had both been racially abused on making their way off the pitch at the end. This was despite the fact that neither Ndlovu, nor the stewards who had to escort Prosser from the field of play, heard anything untoward.

Both an Albion internal inquiry and an FA external inquiry could find no evidence of the apparent racism, with some wondering whether Prosser had exaggerated the missile throwing incident in an attempt to cover up his own ineptitude on the pitch.

One Albion fan captured the majority opinion when he wrote to *The Argus* the following Monday saying: *"Phil Prosser, the referee at the Brighton and Hove Albion versus Sheffield United match on Saturday, was quite simply the worst I have seen in the 12 years I have been supporting the Albion."*

A year later, Mr Prosser drew similar anger from fans, players and officials of Walsall, Derby County and Wigan Athletic. In September 2003 Walsall centre back and former Scotland international Paul Ritchie, faced a lengthy suspension and fine after an incident involving Mr Prosser at Millwall's New Den.

Such was his ire, Ritchie was alleged to have used foul and abusive language and assaulted the official. He had already been cautioned when Prosser showed him a second yellow card in the tunnel for the remarks. Ritchie then allegedly "made contact" with Prosser.

The police took statements from the player and the referee and the incident was reported to the FA and Ritchie was found guilty of foul and abusive language towards the referee.

Less than one month later Mr Prosser won himself few new friends during Derby County's draw with Wigan Athletic at Pride Park.

The game finished 2-2 but the talk after the match was all about Prosser's bizarre decisions which seemed to influence the final score.

Derby centre back Michael Johnson felt particularly hard done by at full time, having been booked for his part in a hard-fought but evenly-contested battle with his ex-Birmingham City team-mate - Wigan striker Geoff Horsfield.

"I asked the ref, 'What do you want, two fairies out there?' After all, this is a man's game and we all have to compete and try to win the ball," Johnson complained.

"Then I went up to him again when he gave that second free kick against me and told him 'This is about two teams trying to play a game of football. People haven't come to watch you'. How did he respond? He booked me!"

The match ended with a total of six bookings, one penalty and an unusually-infuriated Derby manager George Burley, who threw his tracksuit top to the ground in frustration.

"Me and George Burley were doing our heads in on the touchline," Wigan boss Paul Jewell said in a rare display of managerial unity.

"If I have a poor run of matches I get the sack. If a player performs badly for any length of time he gets dropped. But nothing happens to referees if they have a string of bad days at the office," he said.

Tom Finney and I enjoying a splash outside Deepdale

Fans of Burnley later revealed that in the 2003/04 season Prosser had sent off a grand total of 10 players: Iain Anderson (Grimsby), Peter Hawkins (Franchise), Matt Hocking (Boston), Ezomo Iriekpen (Swansea), Paul Ritchie (Walsall), Chris Westwood (Hartlepool), Lee Miller (Bristol City), Karl Munroe (Macclesfield), Danny Harrison (Tranmere) and Leo Roget (Brentford). Incredibly those 10 red cards came in just 19 games and to add to that he had also waved his yellow card on an astounding 81 occasions. He had a run of sending off players in seven successive matches and also waved 53 yellow cards in a run of nine games. But this was nothing new for Prosser, then in his fourth season on the League list, as three of those seasons had been littered with red

157

cards at the rate of one every other game whilst he had already reached 350 yellow cards in that time.

But time passes and near the end of the 2004/05 season, as in 2002, the Albion were struggling in 20th position in the Championship on the back of five straight defeats, and just on point off the relegation places.

Our next fixture was a Tuesday night game away at Deepdale on 5th April 2005 against high flying Preston North End.

And on the day before the match it was announced that the referee was a certain Phil Prosser. There was a sharp intake of breath and together with many Albion fans I began lobbying BHAC chief executive Martin Perry to press the Football Leagues and formally object to Prosser's appointment to referee the game.

But our objections were ignored.

So 36 hours later on a bright and sunny spring evening I drove the 140 miles from my home in South Shields to Preston to cheer on the Albion and see what would unfold.

It was a game to be the proof positive about everything we already knew about Mr Prosser.

In front of a crowd of 14,234, which included about 800 Albion fans gathered high in the Bill Shankley Stand, events unfolded quickly.

Our own line-up that night seemed weak even before kick-off with Adam Blayney in goal and a back four of Joe Dolan, Guy Butters, Dan Harding and striker Gary Hart at right back. There was a five man midfield of Richard Carpenter, Dean Hammond, Nathan Jones, Charlie Oatway and Paul Reid, with Adam Virgo ploughing a loan furrow up front.

It was hardly a line-up to inspire confidence and for the first half an hour we hardly got out of our own half.

But Prosser was yet to strike.

Then in the 24th minute Joe Dolan was booked for a fairly harmless foul and a few minutes later, with Preston laying siege on our 18 yard box, Gary Hart made an innocuous tackle on Prestons' Richard Cresswell a few yards to right of our goal, almost on the touchline.

The home player went down like a sack of coal.

Inside the Preston fortress that is Deepdale

All this happened directly below us and every Brighton supporter in the Bill Shankley Stand had a crystal clear view of the incident. What happened next defied all belief. Prosser immediately blew for a penalty and then sent Hart off, presumably deeming he was the last defender. Quite how he was denying a goal scoring opportunity when the tackle occurred lateral to the goal is to this day unbelievable.

Hart shook his head in disbelief and slowly trudged off the pitch. Graham Alexander duly dispatched the penalty into the top corner, giving Blayney no chance.

The game then became as one-sided as they come, with the Albion not managing a single shot nor corner for the rest of the game. Preston pushed to extend their lead, Sedgwick forcing a good save from Blayney. They doubled their advantage on the stroke of half-time, with Cresswell again involved, turning a cross into the far corner.

North End had the game in the bag within six minutes of the start of the second half when David Nugent guided a low cross into the net.

High in the away stand we knew the game was all over. Chants ran from the gee-up *"We're the right side Brighton boys"* to an amusing but politically incorrect song aimed at the homophobic abuse from the joyous Preston fans: *"I'd rather be a faggot than a chav"* to an ongoing and loud *"Prosser is a Tosser"*.

On the pitch Blayney was a busy man, diving to keep out a shot from Cresswell and then saving superbly to deny Nugent. At the other end, the Preston keeper Carlo Nash had the quietest night that he could have imagined.

Despite the introduction of Leon Knight and Mark McCammon as second half substitutes, there was no way back for the Albion. Paul Reid was booked in the 86th minute which just about summed up the evening for the Albion. The game finished Preston and Prosser 3, Brighton and Hove Albion 0.

The only surprise was that Preston didn't score more.

The defeat also plunged us into an automatic relegation spot with Nottingham Forest and Rotherham with just five games left to play.

It was a long personal drive back to Tyneside that night, but an even longer 280 miles journey for my friends from Sussex.

Some games we will always lose. But thankfully only a few are lost at the moment the referee is appointed.

Brighton and Hove Albion narrowly escaped relegation from the Championship at the end of that 2004/05 season with 51 points and 21 defeats, just one point better off than Gillingham, who were relegated along with Nottingham Forest and Rotherham United. Champions were Sunderland on 94 points with Wigan Athletic as runners-up. Preston North End lost the Play-off final 1-0 to West Ham United.

160

Who Ate All the Pies? Preston

I am unsure if this is sold inside Deepdale, but certainly almost every chip shop, street vendor and café in the vicinity of the ground purveys this delight: Butter Pie – sometimes called Catholic Pie.

It is synonymous with Preston and is a simple pie made from fried onions and potato, with lashings of butter. Often served with chips, if you need the extra cholesterol!

Chapter Seventeen

Anyone Seen Little Cox?
Toddington Services M1
28 March 2008

There is nothing quite like having an intimate moment with your heroes.
The brief encounter happened so unexpectedly, and so publicly. And nothing prepared me for that very personal moment on the M1 motorway, on Friday 28th March 2008.

My dear Aunt Val had died suddenly a few days earlier, and as her next-of-kin I had driven 160 miles from my home in Wrexham to her house in Hemel Hempstead to help sort out her affairs with her solicitor.

My last Albion game had been a couple of weeks earlier, watching us beat Walsall 2-1 at the Bescot Stadium.

But on this day my mind was a million miles away from football or the Albion. Val was my closest relation next to my parents and her death came as a huge shock. So, I guess my mind was focussed on getting everything right and to make plans for her funeral, her orphaned dog - which I had only bought for her a year earlier - and the sale of her large home.

So after going through the basic formalities with her solicitor and the funeral celebrant, I hopped into my car around 1pm to make the long motorway journey back to Wrexham. I stopped at the M1 Toddington Services, just north of Luton, for petrol, a coffee and a toilet break.

Toddington Services on the M1 north of Luton

As I arrived I was vaguely aware of a smart dark coloured coach pulling in next to me in the car park.
But I didn't give it a second glance… what's another coach in a motorway service area anyway?
The loo called first. I really was desperate, so I made my way quickly to the gents, situated away to the left of the cafeteria area. It was a typical motorway mens' toilet with hand-dryers, condom machines and those disconcerting aluminium framed adverts for erectile dysfunction above the urinal trough.
So I stood by the steel trough gazing absent mindedly at one of the adverts, and was just about to relieve myself when it happened.
More than a dozen young guys in dark blue tracksuits and white trainers walked in.

They assembled in various positions either side of me to answer the call of nature.

It was a little bit claustrophobic, but as I started to pee I vaguely looked up at the guy next to me and spontaneously gulped. He had a Brighton and Hove Albion badge on his tracksuit top.

I silently gasped and looked along the urinal at the rest of the guys… it was the entire Brighton first team squad… to my left was our huge keeper Michel Kuipers and to my right was the equally large Tommy Elphick, Joel Lynch and beyond him the diminutive (5ft 4in) Dean Cox… oh and there was our top scorer Nicky Forster too. It was like a Who's Who of the Brighton and Hove Albion 2007/08 squad!

This was the OMG moment when I got instant water retention and the adverts for erectile dysfunction and cheap car insurance were a distant memory, as a voice in my head yelled: *"Stop looking at them… stop looking at them… stop looking at them!"*

I was peeing with my heroes… or in my case I was not. I couldn't even get a drop out!

I speedily moved to wash and dry my hands, hoping none of the players had noticed me looking… but I felt I had to say something. So as I exited the toilets I turned to the player coming out next to me – our full back Andrew Whing – and politely asked: *"What are you guys doing in Luton?"*

"We are on our way to Leeds, we play them tomorrow," was the polite reply.

"Do we?" I answered stupidly, still desperate for a wee, as manager Dean Wilkins and Dean White strolled in smiling.

With a resigned: *"Thanks… and good luck"* and in a star-struck daze I walked over to the food service area grinning from ear to ear.

"I am 52 years old, for Christ sake," I said to myself, *"I shouldn't be feeling star-struck like this about some bloody footballers!"*

I actually laughed out loud.

I ordered my coffee and a sandwich, and out of the corner of my eye watched the Albion players grab some isotonic drinks for the remainder of their journey.

Then with a sudden realisation I quietly cursed: *"They didn't even know I was a Brighton and Hove Albion supporter… how could they!"*

Albion midfielder Dean Cox © The Argus

I continued my own journey home with the moment rattling around my head.

As I pulled into my driveway I suddenly laughed out loud: *"If only I had said: Has anyone seen little Cox?"*

Hmm, or maybe not!

Brighton and Hove Albion fought out a 0-0 draw at Elland Road the next day in front of 22,575 fans. In the Albion team that day were Michel Kuipers, Kerry Mayo, Andrew Whing, Joel Lynch and Tommy Elphick. Dean Cox was the motor of midfield alongside three players probably forgotten by many Albion supporters: David Martot, Therry Racon and Steve Thomson, while up front were Nicky Forster and a young Glenn Murray.

By coincidence the Leeds keeper that day was Casper Ankergren, who two years later joined the Albion and made 68 appearances for us.

The 2007/08 campaign had got off to the best possible start off the pitch, with the club receiving news that the government had granted permission for Albion's move to Falmer.

On the pitch, Nicky Forster arrived at the club in a £75,000 move from Hull City, while Andrew Whing, who had enjoyed a loan spell, signed permanently from Coventry City. Forster consistently found the back of the net during the opening half of the season, and Albion were just outside the play-off positions after the first 20 games.

But a poor run of form followed and a number of key players departed in January, including skipper Dean Hammond, Bas Savage and striker Alex Revell.

Heading in the other direction was Steve Thomson - a central midfielder from Falkirk - and also arriving at the Withdean Stadium was Rochdale's Glenn Murray, a £300,000 striker.

Murray hit the ground running with two goals on his debut against Crewe, which triggered an upturn in form for the Seagulls, as they began to climb the league table again.

But following that draw away to Leeds United, a disappointing 3-2 home defeat to Port Vale followed and Albion's chances of reaching the League One play-offs faded.

The Seagulls ended the campaign with three victories in their last four games, but it wasn't enough to finish inside the top six, as they finished just outside, trailing Southend by seven points.

The intimate moment with my Albion heroes in the M1 Toddington Services in 2008 reminds me of something quite similar some 167 miles away in 1989. At the time I was working as an assistant editor for a series of glossy computer magazines at Addlington Park, near Stockport.

On a bright spring day I popped downstairs in our newly built office complex to answer the call of nature.

As I began to open the toilet door I was aware of someone pushing the door on the other side. Suddenly I was face to face with the unmistakable Scotland and Manchester United legend Denis Law.

I gasped: *"Denis Law!"*
He smiled and replied: *"Aye, that's me lad"* before disappearing upstairs.
I later got to the bottom of why he was there. Denis was working with his former team-mate and friend Francis Lee in his paper recycling and toilet paper manufacturing business FH Lee Ltd – a company which made Lee a multi-millionaire after retiring from playing football in 1976.
Denis Law was visiting our magazine company to sell us toilet rolls and other stationery.

Brighton and Hove Albion ended the 2007/08 season in League One in 7th place with 69 points. Champions that year were Swansea City on 92 points and runners up were Nottingham Forest.
Leeds United finished that season in 5th place with 76 points after being given a 15 point deduction after going into administration the previous season. They lost the League One Play-Final 1-0 to Doncaster Rovers. Without that points deduction Leeds would have been automatically promoted.

Who Ate All the Pies? Luton

I won't spoil the content flow of this book with a picture of a Toddington Services motorway coffee and a cardboard sandwich.
But nearby Luton Town for me is forever associated with spicy Keema-filled Naan and Donner Kebabs. I doubt I have ever seen so many kebab vans near a football ground than at Kenilworth Road!

Chapter Eighteen

Tears Before Bed Time
The Racecourse
7 January 2012

My son Nathan regaled for the big game

The events of the Fans United game at Wrexham's Racecourse in November 2004 will always remain with me for so many reasons, both personal and professional.

That spontaneous decision to phone BBC Radio Five Live a month earlier to highlight Wrexham's plight set a ball rolling that became wholly life changing. From a football/professional perspective it was a rollercoaster ride which never looked like stopping... at times scary, but also exhilarating:

- First there was the cold Friday evening on 3rd December 2004, when Wrexham had been drawn against Scunthorpe

United in the second round of the FA Cup at the Iron's Glanford Park. I had arranged to attend the game because it was poignant for many reasons. This was the day Wrexham FC was placed into receivership and faced a winding-up petition. It was also a match which was being shown live on Sky TV. And in an act of reciprocal friendship the Wrexham fans had produced a huge **Wrexham 4 Falmer** banner. Much to the shock of the home fans, they had also showered the goal area with blue and white balloons just before kick-off.

The Wrexham 4 Falmer banner at Scunthorpe

- Then there was a **Clubs in Crisis** game, for which I had arranged publicity on a chilly 29th January 2005 (the reverse fixture against Doncaster Rovers). This attracted more than 6,000 supporters to highlight the plight of many clubs in the English leagues who were facing receivership or ruination due to rogue owners – Grimsby Town, Rotherham, Leeds United and Cambridge United were well represented.

- Next was a huge personal surprise when I was nominated for and won BBC Radio Five Live's Football Fan of the Year for 2004. As well as a VIP visit to the Victoria Derbyshire show at Broadcasting House in London, it also triggered a series of live TV and radio interviews, press coverage and a lovely spontaneous phone call from Albion chief executive Martin Perry to congratulate me.
- Then came another Fans United day on the 19th March 2005 at Cambridge United's Abbey Stadium to highlight how close they were to extinction. It was a day when Wrexham and Brighton supporters mobbed the home stand while Ipswich and Norwich fans rubbed shoulders with each other. At the break I was suddenly invited to speak on BBC Five Live's half time report about the crisis facing many clubs outside the top flight.

"FIT AND PROPER" TOUR 1997 - ?

08/02/97 **Brighton & Hove Albion**
Goldstone Ground

14/02/98 **Doncaster Rovers**
Priestfield Stadium, Gillingham

15/01/99 **Chester City**
Deva Stadium

28/03/99 **Portsmouth**
Fratton Park

16/12/01 **Wimbledon**
Selhurst Park

02/02/02 **York City**
Bootham Crescent

20/11/04 **Wrexham**
Racecourse Ground

19/03/05 **Cambridge United**
Abbey Stadium

??/??/?? **YOUR CLUB HERE...?**
Grounds For Action!

A memento of the Fans United day at Cambridge United's Abbey Stadium

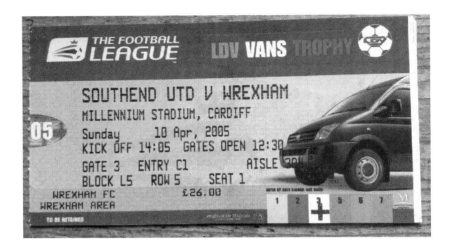

- And in a cruel twist of fate, while Wrexham were struggling for survival, the Dragons made it to the LDV Final on 10th April 2005, at the Millennium Stadium in Cardiff, in front of a crowd of 36,216, including at least a dozen Albion fans. More TV and radio interviews followed, while Wrexham won the trophy with a handsome 2-0 victory against Southend.

- Then finally the accolade which in hindsight means the most. At Wrexham's end of season AGM of their Supporters Trust on 16th June, their chairman proposed a "special mention" for "Nic Outerside (sic) - For his outstanding PR work in promoting the plight of Wrexham FC."

This was some rollercoaster ride.

But life has a cruel way of kicking you in the teeth. And something had to give. While I was so deeply involved with Fans United, Brighton, Wrexham and football in general, my wife had found comfort with another man.

When I discovered the truth in October of 2005, I knew I had already lost her and the marriage for good.

In a twisted irony, my parents who had been married for 55 years, were also facing a tough time, with my father suffering from the later stages of Parkinson's disease.

Wrexham friend Neil Roberts and I at the LDV Final in Cardiff

Mum had decided she couldn't cope with nursing my dad alone, so put their house up for sale with a plan to move to North Wales to be close to both my sisters.

For me, with the trauma of a broken marriage, a move south to Wales from Tyneside seemed the only option. By early January 2006, and with my 50th birthday imminent, I secured a weekly newspaper editor's job, initially in Welshpool and later in Mold. Everything seemed in place and fate determined that I find a house in the Wrexham area.

By April of 2006, I was a 24/7 single parent to my youngest son Nathan, who had only just turned four and was ensconced in the former pit village of Coedpoeth, just a mile from Wrexham town centre.

The spring and summer was a blur of settling to a new life, new job and new parenting responsibilities while dealing with a divorce and being made bankrupt by my ex-wife's refusal to pay her half of the mortgage on our old home.

But by September my new life had really begun and I had enrolled Nathan at a small local primary school in Bwlchgwyn.

The following six years were an ongoing matter of personal survival, raising a bright and active son alone, editing a thriving newspaper, going to as many Albion away games in the North West and West Midlands as I could fit in, and taking in a fair number of Wrexham home games too.

One highlight was watching them on a sunny May afternoon in 2007 face Boston United in an end of season contest as crucial as our own last game at Hereford had been 10 years earlier. In front of a sell-out crowd of 12,374, only a win for Wrexham would keep them in the Football League at the expense of their opponents Boston. A draw or loss would send them down. And just like that Hereford decider in 1997, Wrexham went in at half time 1-0 down. But the rollercoaster didn't stop rolling and an exhilarating second half saw them run out 3-1 winners. And there was me resplendent in my blue and white stripes, jumping for joy and hugging Wrexham fans around me!

The joy was short-lived and with ongoing financial struggles, Wrexham were eventually relegated from the Football League exactly one year later, finishing rock bottom of League Two at the end of the 2007/08 season behind their bitter rivals Chester City. Meanwhile, my son Nathan was not only learning to speak Welsh he was also turning into a Wrexham fan.

Then suddenly in December 2011, everything made sense again in life and football.

By this time, Wrexham had been languishing in non-league football for almost four years, while the Albion, under Gus Poyet, were in the ascendancy, in our sparkling new stadium at Falmer and having a good season in the Championship.

The juxtaposition of fortunes between our respective clubs could not be clearer.

Then it happened… I walked into work at about 8am on Monday 5th December, bracing myself for the typical busy Christmas run-in of producing three consecutive newspapers with a skeleton staff (due to festive season holidays) when I was stopped in my tracks.

My good friend and associate editor Martin Wright, who is a lifelong Wrexham fan, was beaming across his face.

"Well what do you think of the FA Cup draw, Nic?" he demanded.

I was bemused, as due to parenting duties, the 2nd round of the FA Cup had passed me by.

Flummoxed I simply answered: *"Why?"*

I was soon to discover that after despatching Brentford away at Griffin Park, Wrexham had drawn Brighton and Hove Albion in the 3rd round at the Amex Stadium!

I gave a polite *"whoop"* in the quiet newsroom as Martin said: *"What a game for both of us!"*

The match was scheduled for Saturday 7th January… just one month away.

My run-up to Christmas was spent with the usual seasonal festivities, pressurised work and arranging child care for Nathan for the weekend of 6th/8th January. Plus also gently explaining to my son that I could not get tickets and a hotel room for both of us. I had obtained a ticket for one in the west stand.

As the weeks passed, it was clear that this game was big for us, but even bigger for Wrexham.

By New Year it was evident that more than 2,000 Wrexham fans planned to travel to Brighton by planes, trains and automobiles to ensure they witnessed this occasion.

More than 12 coaches were also scheduled to start out at 8am on the Saturday morning for the long haul to the south coast as excitement was becoming intense.

On the Friday I drove the 252 miles to Brighton and found a beautiful overnight lodging at a small hotel in Kemp Town.

The Saturday could not dawn fast enough, and after a trawl around North Laine, some music CD shopping and a pizza, I made my way to our beloved stadium.

The 18,573 crowd was buzzing. The stadium was only two-thirds full, but the fans of both sides more than made up for it with noise… mutual admiration and vocal support for our own teams. There was even time for an on-field presentation by the Wrexham Supporters Trust to Brighton and Hove Albion in recognition of our support during their crisis some eight years earlier.

The match kicked off in a vibrant atmosphere, with the Albion holding possession but Wrexham always threatening on the break. A mistake by visiting keeper Mayebi handed us an early opportunity to assert superiority - but Kazenga LuaLua could only direct his shot across the face of goal.

Wrexham gradually settled into the game, with Jake Speight's pace in particular causing problems for our captain for the day, Inigo Calderon.

Both sides were playing an open, expansive game and only a last-ditch tackle from Matt Sparrow denied Speight following Morrell's cross. A long-range effort by LuaLua flew past the post before Speight twice went close at the other end.

Having held out for 45 minutes, Wrexham conceded only 90 seconds into the second half with Jake Forster-Caskey tapping in LuaLua's precise cross from the byline.

But then having provided the assist for the goal, LuaLua was forced off the field five minutes later with a hamstring injury and was replaced by Toby Agdestein.

Wrexham refused to buckle and they were level on 62 minutes. Anton Rodgers had a chance to restore Brighton's lead but it would have been harsh on Wrexham who had shown plenty of endeavour. The Wrexham players were applauded off the field at the end of the game.

It was a match to remember… but better was still to come!

The replay was scheduled for Tuesday 17th January at the Racecourse and my first thought was I had to take Nathan, or he would never forgive me.

So on Monday (9th January) morning I told my son that I was getting tickets for us both.

"But dad I don't want to sit with the Brighton fans, I might get mugged wearing red!" he replied, with a huge grin on his face.

That was my dilemma.

But after a brief phone call to a friend who was a senior member of the Wrexham Supporters Trust, the problem was easily solved.

"The away support is housed in the far end of the Family Stand," he explained. *"What I'll do is get you both seats at the far right of the Wrexham section, so you are sitting next to the Brighton support."*

So tickets collected, we waited for the following Tuesday to arrive as we watched the winter weather close in. The weekend was freezing cold and there was heavy snow. By Monday (16th January) it was touch and go whether the game would go ahead. And by Tuesday afternoon the match was officially postponed due to a frozen pitch. This caused problems for many Albion fans who had either booked transport, overnight accommodation or time off work for the replay.

But a slight overnight thaw meant the game would be played the following day on Wednesday 18th January.
I had rarely witnessed such excitement from my son as I did when I told him the news.
"It is so great, dad, cos my teacher and almost everyone in my class is going to be there!" he smiled.
So early on Wednesday evening, father and son dressed very differently. Nathan was wrapped in red, with his Wrexham shirt and scarf and a Wales anorak, while I wore my regulation blue and white stripes, Albion scarf and my bright blue ski jacket. Both of us had gloves and wore extra layers – I had learned a bitter lesson from Grimsby eight years earlier!

I drove the one mile to the ground and parked in a nearby retail park car park. Both laughing, we walked the short distance to outside the Mold Road Stand to meet a few friends.

"Dad, I am so hungry," Nathan suddenly blurted, on noticing the burger and hot dog vans.

We were already getting a few looks and smiles from Wrexham supporters as we walked toward the smell of fried onions and chips, as a Sky TV team followed us with their cameras.

I took Nathan to the first van and ordered two pies and two portions of chips. As I held out a tenner to pay for the food, the woman running the van held up her hand in a stop motion. *"They're free,"* she said. *"It's a thank you for coming tonight and for everything you have done."*

I felt tears welling in my eyes as I held Nathan's hand and walked him round to the other side of the ground.

Everywhere we walked there were more smiles and hellos from Wrexham supporters I barely recognised. When we got to the home turnstile in the Yale Stand a bigger shock was in store. While I watched Nathan safely through the junior entrance I tried to explain to the guy operating the adult turnstile that although I was a Brighton supporter I was there with my young son.

"There's no need to explain," the guy replied, *"We all know who you are. You'll never be forgotten in these parts."*

And as he saw me through the turnstile the tears began to flow.

"What's up dad?" asked a worried looking Nathan, when I caught up with him under the stand.

"Nothing, just happy tears," I replied.

"I don't know why you're happy," he laughed, *"We're gonna beat you tonight,"* he added, while kicking my right leg.

So we made our way to our seats high in the stand, with me sat on the far right and Nathan next to me alongside a melee of Wrexham supporters as part of a bumper 8,316 crowd, which was huge considering the whole Kop end was closed off due to health and safety breaches.

By kick-off the atmosphere was electric.

Inigo Calderon was captain for the evening and in front of Peter Brezovan in goal the starting XI was a strong side compared to the

178

youngsters blooded in the first game at the Amex. In central defence Grant Hall was partnered with Lewis Dunk, Romain Vincelot at left back, with a midfield of Liam Bridcutt, Alan Navarro and Matt Sparrow, with Will Buckley out wide. Our goal threat was a combination of Craig MacKail-Smith and Will Hoskins.

As the game kicked off the atmosphere inside our stand was bubbling. Matt Sparrow was the first to try his luck on goal inside the opening three minutes when his shot from outside the area flew past Mayebi's left-hand post.

But the Dragons also made a positive start and player manager Andy Morrell's effort from six yards out was blocked by Brezovan.

Then on 23 minutes the unthinkable happened...following a strong run down the left, Danny Wright found Morrell on the edge of the area and his powerful curling shot found the top right corner of the goal.

Nathan was screaming and yelling as I felt him disappear. I turned in shock to find the middle-aged Wrexham guy behind him holding my son aloft. *"Sorry mate, but he can't see the celebrations,"* the man explained.

As Nathan sat back in his seat, he punched me softly in the ribs and shouted: *"Told you we're gonna win."*

Wrexham's defence kept things tight at the other end and we were still trailing at half-time.

As the second half got underway we were finding it hard to get a grip of the game and Will Hoskins fired over the crossbar from inside the area following Will Buckley's quickly taken free-kick.

The home side were pressing for a second goal but against the run of play, Albion substitute Ashley Barnes equalised with a powerful header from outside the six yard box.

So it was 1-1 at 90 minutes and the game continued to fluctuate for the 30 minutes of extra time.

Next to me a weary 10-year-old boy was still running on adrenalin as we moved to a penalty shoot-out and the deadlock was at last broken when Dean Keates saw his effort saved by Brezovan.

Both sides successfully converted their next four penalties before Craig Mackail-Smith hammered home his spot-kick to secure a fourth-round home tie with Newcastle United at the Amex.

Craig Mackail-Smith hammers home the Albion's winning penalty

The defeat was harsh on the last non-league side left in the competition, who had more than matched their Championship opponents.

And as we left the stand to wend our short distance home, Nathan turned to me with tears in his eyes, and in words that will always stay lodged in my memory forever, said: *"We were robbed."*

Brighton and Hove Albion went on to beat Newcastle 1-0 in the 4th Round of the FA Cup before crashing out 6-1 to Liverpool at Anfield in the 5th Round.
We finished the 2011/2012 season in 10th position in the Championship on 66 points. Champions that year were Reading on 89 points with Southampton as runners-up.

Who Ate All the Pies? Wrexham

You can't visit a Wrexham game without trying a pie from the nearby *Village Bakery* in Coedpoeth. These rich deep-filled short crust pastries, pasties, and pies are sold at the Racecourse and in almost every store in the area. Hot or cold you'll come back for a second one.

Chapter Nineteen

Is This a Fire Drill?
Vale Park
25 January 2014

I guess it had to happen! Some 34 years after I took my first
wife to her first football match in Leeds, for her to vow she
would never go again; I was now about to escort my new
significant other to her own **Brighton and Hove Albion
baptism.**

Gill and I had married the previous February and although she
wasn't strictly a football virgin – she had been in the directors' box
at Nottingham Forest during the Clough years to quaff prawn
sandwiches and champagne - she had never been on the terraces of
any football ground.

We were both entering unchartered territory in our marriage.

So the event was planned with meticulous precision, to try and ensure that football wasn't going to spoil another marriage.

I had picked a 4th Round FA Cup tie away at League One Port Vale – then managed by Micky Adams – in a game which I felt sure we would win, and in which there was no bitter rivalry. The fact that Burslem was only 26 miles from our home in Whitchurch added to the ease of the occasion.

During the week leading up to the match I tried a bit of simple soccer mansplaining: the league structure, the names of key Albion players, a little about our manager Oscar Garcia, why a referee might hand out yellow and red cards, penalty kicks and the fact the teams change ends at half-time… I even tried to use a shopping analogy to explain the offside rule.

I also gave my wife plenty of warnings regarding the language she might hear on the terraces and that prawn sandwiches and champagne were not on the menu, neither were cushioned seats, nor set intermissions for comfort breaks.

I need not have worried, because that day at Vale Park I realised a new depth to our marriage and my wife.

Around noon on Saturday 25th January 2014, and wrapped up warm for the cold weather, we set off to drive the short journey to the Potteries.

We knew we were almost there when waiting at traffic lights, between the red brick terraces of Burslem, two guys wearing the black and white of Port Vale walked past both eating cheese and oatcakes from a paper wrapping.

"Blimey, what the hell are they munching on?" Gill exclaimed.

So as I drove the half mile to a car park near the ground I explained that melted cheese in rolled Staffordshire Oatcakes were a staple diet in this area – something I had discovered over many trips to both Port Vale and Stoke City. I then promised to buy some Oatties and cook them for breakfast the next day.

Okay, I over-mansplained!

On arrival at Vale Park we quickly collected our tickets from the ticket office under the watchful gaze of the amazing Roy Sproson bronze statue.

Sproson was a one-club Port Vale legend who made 842 appearances for Vale between 1950 and 1972. He later managed the club for three years.

So with tickets safely in our pockets, Gill looked at me and asked: *"Where can we get food?"* I pointed nervously towards two vans parked close to the away entrance at the Signal One Stand.

We both walked towards the nearest food retailer, but their fayre was limited to burgers, hot dogs, chips and pies.

"So where are these famous oatcakes?" asked Gill.

I looked back blankly before ordering hot dogs for both of us.

I was munching my way into my roll when I noticed my wife pulling a strange face next to me.

"What's up?" I enquired.

"They call this food… it is revolting," Gill replied as she handed me the rest of her hot dog.

So we made our way through the turnstile and into the concourse behind and below the old stand.

I looked around and saw a food and drink stall to our right, and suggested I get us both a Bovril and see if they have other food options.

Gill stared daggers at me. *"I hate Bovril and I don't want to go down with salmonella before the match starts,"* she stated with a dismissive smile.

So I bought myself a piping hot Bovril and my wife a lidded cup of tea and we made our way to our seats about half way back in the stand.

We chatted and laughed and checked our watches. There was still over 45 minutes to kick-off but in front of us the weather was changing, with a cold wind and rain blowing across the pitch.

Then suddenly the whole ground darkened and the sound of what seemed like machine gun bullets rattled the roof of the stand. Before us visibility was down to 30 feet as the most violent hail storm swept across the pitch. The hail went on for more than 10 minutes and lay like a white sheet across the grass. I feared that it might lead to the match being abandoned. But as quickly as it arrived the storm passed.

Next to me Gill said: *"I've been thinking while watching the hail… do they allow you to take your own food to football grounds?"*

The hail storm across Vale Park 45 minutes before kick-off

I looked at her blankly for the second time that afternoon.
"I think so," I replied, *"Although I've never tried."*
"Well I am going to pack a picnic for the next game we go to," Gill exclaimed.
My head was buzzing… blimey the game hadn't even started and my new wife was talking about going again! I squeezed her hand and smiled broadly.
Around us our stand was filling up with travelling Albion fans and some diverse chants were being bedded in. In the other stands Vale fans were also starting to arrive.
Soon the match day squads were out warming up and I sat pointing out various players to watch to my wife.
The Albion side had a distinct second XI feel about it – hardly surprising considering that promotion was our main and realistic objective that season. So with second choice Peter Brezovan in goal and youngsters Adam Chicksen, Rohan Ince, Jake Forster-Caskey and Solly March in the starting XI, plus out of form Kemy Agustien in midfield and loanee Jonathan Okika up front there was a feeling

that this might be a tighter game than we thought. And why was Leonardo Ulloa on the bench? Only Matt Upson, Lewis Dunk and Andrea Orlandi gave any substance to the line-up… at least on paper.

Meanwhile around us, more than 1,100 Albion fans had filled the Signal One Stand (out of an official attendance of 7,293) and the chanting was in full throttle… and yes we were going through the full repertoire!

As the game kicked off in atrocious driving rain I could hear my wife chuckling next to me.

"Which one is Oscar Garcia who drinks sangria?" she asked

So as I explained that he was our Spanish manager, another rendition of: *"Oscar Garcia, He drinks sangria, He came from Barca, To bring us joy, He's got stubble, Like Barney Rubble, So please don't take my Oscar away!"* started up.

With that, a new chant of *"We've got a big Pole in our goal,"* started. I could sense Gill staring at our giant Slovak keeper Brezovan and quickly explained that the chant related to our first choice Polish keeper Tomasz Kuszczak, who wasn't even a substitute that day, but had been chatting to fans at the front of our stand.

"Why is he out of favour?" asked my wife before I mansplained the need to rest some players for cup games and to blood some of the younger players.

We started the game strongly with Lewis Dunk shooting narrowly wide after a purposeful run and March tested Vale's keeper Neal with a fierce strike.

The Albion were dominating possession and deservedly took the lead in the 27th minute when one of our youngsters Rohan Ince hooked a half volley from an Orlandi corner into the Vale net.

The Albion fans were delirious, while the rest of the ground fell deathly quiet.

Immediately the supporters around us started the usual chanting of *"Is this a library?"* and the more pointed *"There's no one there."*

Next to me Gill was laughing out loud.

"I love the songs," she said, *"Even if I can't make out all the words… they're hilarious."*

I mused back to my early games at the Goldstone and how it took me months to get the *"Cha Cha Cha Liveseee"* chant right and how years later I often messed up *"When the ball hits the net.... it's Zamora"* song and felt sympathy.

Orlandi challenges for a ball as Matt Upson looks on   © The Sentinel

Then suddenly while I was musing and my wife listening to the chanting, Vale's Chris Robertson headed an equaliser from six yards. Game on!

But there was still time for the Seagulls to regain the lead before the interval and, although it was arguably deserved, the goal was actually quite bizarre.

Solly March tried to send in a cross from the right but appeared to miscue his attempted centre and the ball floated into the far top corner of the Vale net with the keeper stranded. In hindsight the goal was reminiscent of his equaliser five years later against Millwall in the Quarter Final of the FA Cup!

March's strike seemed to end the home side's hopes and the Albion were barely troubled after the interval.

But not before our crowd teased the Port Vale fans. As they began chanting: *"Micky Adams black and white army"*, our fans responded: *"Micky Adams blue and white army."* Micky waved to both sets of fans as I explained the significance of the chants to Gill.

We had several chances to make the game safe after the half-time break.

March tested Neal with a decent strike seconds into the second half and the home keeper then made a superb save from Jake Forster-Caskey's dipping long-range effort.

Neal also made a brilliant diving stop to deny Kemy Agustien, tipping the midfielder's fizzing low strike onto the post.

Obika rolls the ball into an empty net for Albion's third goal

Former Albion player Doug Loft also had a decent strike that went just wide for Vale. But with 12 minutes remaining Obika added a third for the Seagulls when he latched on to a through ball and calmly rounded Neal and tapped the ball into an empty net. His celebratory salute to our fans was weird to say the least.

At this point large sections of the home crowd started to make their way out of the ground. And the Brighton fans launched into *"Is This a Fire Drill?"* By this time Gill was laughing even louder next to me and shouting in my right ear: *"This is so funny... it's brilliant."*

So the Albion were winners 3-1 and faced Hull City in the Fifth Round, where we succumbed 2-1 in a replay at the KC Stadium.

On the short drive home my first question to my wife was: *"Well did you enjoy it?"*

Her answer was concise: *"The food was shit and I didn't follow all the football... but the chanting, the songs and the atmosphere was amazing. And I didn't hear anyone swear once... when is the next game we can go to?"*

I swear she wasn't really listening!

Brighton and Hove Albion finished 6th in the Championship in the 2013/14 season with 72 points, losing out to Derby County in the Play-off semi-final. Champions were Leicester City with 102 points, with Burnley also promoted as runners-up.

Who Ate All the Pies? Port Vale

There is a football foodstuff unique to Port Vale, Stoke City and all the amateur clubs in the Potteries, simply known as Staffordshire Oatcakes. These floppy pancake-looking oat breads are rolled and heated with cheese inside and often as a breakfast with cheese and bacon. They are just delicious!

Chapter Twenty

Bribing the Blues
St Andrews
5 April 2016

It is strange that in football what goes around often comes around.
It is also strange that my wife Gill feels a need to smuggle food into every football match she ever goes to.
Port Vale's catering still has a lot to answer for!
Just like other fans, Gill is not allowed to take plastic bottles of water into most grounds anymore, but that doesn't stop her filling

her shoulder-bag with sandwiches, cakes, pickled gherkins, rice pudding and home-made flapjack.

And it is the last of these items which saved our lives – well at least our seats – at an Albion game in Birmingham in the spring of 2016. With my youngest son – then aged 14 – on his Easter break, my wife had surprised us all by buying three tickets for a Tuesday evening promotion run-in game at Biirmingham City's St Andrew's ground.

It was - at least on paper – an all-ticket match. And it was to be my son Nathan's first Brighton game since the FA Cup replay at Wrexham way back in January 2012.

I was doubly delighted as I had tried since the previous Saturday to get tickets from the Amex ticket office, only to be told they were sold out.

So after kissing my wife with gratitude, I checked that the tickets were for the Gil Merrick stand – which usually houses the away supporters.

They were… and in Block Six.

Before the game the Albion were third in the Championship table on 72 points, chasing Burnley and Middlesbrough occupying the automatic promotion places on 76 and 73 points respectively.

So a win at St Andrew's that warm April evening was vital to Brighton's own promotion hopes

At 6pm on Tuesday 5th April and clad in Albion blue the three of us set off for the game.

But the 18-mile drive from our home in Wolverhampton to Small Heath in the east end of Birmingham that sunny evening was a nightmare. Due to roadworks and rush hour traffic on the M6, a journey which normally takes 35 minutes took double that time.

On arrival we hurriedly parked in a rough-hewn car park about 800 yards from the ground, exchanged pleasantries with a few Birmingham City fans and walked briskly to the ticket office on Cattell Road. On being given our tickets, enclosed in a sealed envelope, we then had to walk around almost the entire ground to find the entrance to our stand. The guy at the turnstile hardly looked up as he scanned our tickets and ushered us through to Block Six.

We took seats near the front, just as the two teams made their way out from the tunnel a few yards to our left.

It was a strong line-up that night with Stockdale in goal, a back four of Bruno, Connor Goldson, Lewis Dunk and Liam Rosenior, the steady midfield pairing of Dale Stephens and Beram Kayal, with Jiri Skalak and Kazenga Lua Lua out wide and Steve Sidwell playing in an attacking midfield role just behind Tomer Hemed.

But one thing became unnervingly obvious to the three of us before the game kicked off - that the bulk of Albion supporters were at least two blocks away to our right and we seemed to be sitting in a neutral zone which had filled up with families and kids.

"Maybe it's for both sets of supporters," my son suggested.

I pulled the match ticket from my inside jacket pocket and studied it carefully – it certainly had Gil Merrick Stand Block 6 printed on it. Surely not a mistake?

But there had been a mistake, and it became blindingly obvious when on 16 minutes Kyle Lafferty scored a surprise opener for the Blues.

At that point, everyone around us (and I mean everyone!) stood up and cheered and chanted Lafferty's name.

We sat stony faced as chants of *"Albion, Albion"* echoed 50 yards to the right.

"Fuck it, we are in the wrong stand," I whispered to my wife.

Then as sure as night follows day, at the other end of the pitch the Albion quickly levelled as Connor Goldson netted his first goal for the club, heading in a pin point Jiri Skalak free-kick from 12 yards.

I was on my feet cheering wildly, before I felt a gentle female hand pull me down to my seat.

Gill was looking beyond me at two match stewards who were walking purposefully towards us from the pitch side hoardings.

"Is that a Brighton shirt you're wearing, Sir?" asked the first steward, pointing at the hem of my shirt hanging below my zippered jacket.

"Can I see your tickets?" asked the second steward, with an enquiring look on his face..

Behind me I could hear my son say: *"Shit, dad, we've got the wrong tickets."*

Albion players celebrate Connor Goldson's first goal © BHAFC

The first steward then said: *"You're in the wrong end my friend, you're gonna have to leave."*
I tried to explain that we lived in Wolverhampton and the ticket office must have assumed by our postcode that we were Birmingham fans.
"Sorry, I know you have been behaving well, but we are going to have to eject you," added the second steward.
And it was at this moment my wife spun some feminine magic, which I can only smile back on as totally inspired.
Reaching deep into her handbag she retrieved two large pieces of home-made flapjack and with a smile on her face said: *"Would you two gentlemen like a piece of my flapjack?"* Before adding: *"My parents live in Solihull* (on the eastern outskirts of Birmingham) *and it's my mum's own recipe."*
Both the Brummy stewards smiled in reply, and the second one said: *"That's very kind of you… thank you."* And as he took a piece of flapjack, he politely added: *"Will you please come with us."* So we followed the young burly guys up to back of the enclosure,

expecting them to escort us to the exit gates. But on passing through one set of doors, the first steward turned and said: *"We shouldn't really do this but we can get you into Block 4 where your Brighton friends are."*

We passed through two more set of steel doors before we were ushered politely to three seats midway back in the Brighton and Hove Albion section.

I turned and the second steward winked at me and said: *"Enjoy the game Sir, we are going off to enjoy your missus' flapjack."*

A young Birmingham City steward probably hoping for a piece of flapjack! Former Albion keeper Tomasz Kuszczak looks on

I quickly hugged Gill and whispered: *"You are a star; that was inspired."*
She laughed: *"The way to a man's heart is always through his stomach!"*
Meanwhile, on the pitch, the Albion had gained the impetus and we were putting waves of pressure on the Birmingham goal.

Half-time was a blur of Bovril, tea and crisps all round after Gill explained she had eaten the last piece of flapjack herself.

Then three minutes after the break Lewis Dunk kept the Albion's automatic promotion hopes alive with a crucial winner.

Maikel Kieftenbeld gifted us a needless corner and Dunk arrived unmarked to thump in an eight-yard header from Skalak's centre. The celebrations were wild as the players sucked in our cheers and chanting just a few feet in front of where we were now standing. We all shared a belief that this would be our year.

Two minutes later former Albion keeper Tomasz Kuszczak denied Tomer Hemed a spectacular third, turning away the striker's overhead kick, after the Seagulls had cut Birmingham apart.

Brighton were never troubled again and Jamie Murphy could have added the gloss with two minutes left only for Blues defender Morrison to block his 12-yard effort.

Manchester United loanee James Wilson almost made it 3-1 in added time when he broke from a corner but, with Kuszczak stranded up field, he failed to beat Birmingham City's right back Paul Caddis.

The final whistle blew to delight all around us, most of us celebrating to applaud our players. Even Gill wanted to stay to applaud them.

The drive home was a lot quicker and happier than the outward journey had been just two hours earlier.

Once sat in our living room with a beer and a glass of wine we all laughed at how two pieces of flapjack had saved the day.

"What shall I take next time?" Gill quipped, as I hoped she wasn't going for the pickled gherkins again!

The Albion's win that night kept us on track, but with Middlesbrough winning 3-0 at home and Burnley drawing 0-0 it was still a case of playing catch-up for the automatic promotion berths.

It is ironic that as I write this chapter in March 2019, three years after that game, a storm has erupted around Birmingham City and the stewarding of its home games.

A Birmingham City fan was jailed for 14 weeks for physically attacking Aston Villa captain Jack Grealish during the second city derby.

Paul Mitchell, of Rubery, Worcestershire, ran on to the pitch past stewards and hit Grealish from behind about 10 minutes into the game.

Mitchell, 27, admitted assault and encroachment on to the pitch at Birmingham Magistrates' Court. He was also ordered to pay £350 in fines and costs and has been banned from attending any football matches in the UK for 10 years. Birmingham City apologised to both Grealish and Villa immediately after the game and said Mitchell had been banned from St Andrew's for life.

The club said there were *"no excuses"* for his behaviour, which *"has no place in football".*

But in a separate development at the same game a match day steward was involved in an altercation in which he appeared to push Jack Grealish after the Villa star went into the crowd to celebrate his 67th minute winner at St Andrews.

Birmingham opened an investigation into the incident, which was caught on camera, and said they would review all of their *"stewarding, safety and security procedures as a matter of high importance."*

But we already knew that a crafty piece of flapjack would always win!

Brighton and Hove Albion finished the 2015/16 season in 3rd place in the Championship on 89 points, just behind second placed Middlesbrough, but only on a single goal difference. Champions were Burnley on 93 points.

The Albion eventually lost their play-off semi-final against Sheffield Wednesday, with a depleted side and despite a spirited second leg at the Amex.

Hull City were promoted via the play-offs.

Who Ate All the Pies? Birmingham

It would be easy to feature a piece of flapjack here. But there are many wonderful options for footie food in the area around Small Heath and south east Birmingham, which is the heart of the Second City's South Asian communities: curries, keema wraps, hot and cold street food and Balti pies abound. Or just a spicy Pakora and a Samosa, as pictured here.

Chapter Twenty-One

Football's Coming Home
Molineux
14 April 2017

The main Stan Cullis Stand at Molineux, constructed by the Buckingham Group who also built the Amex Stadium

And so it came to pass… and to mix allegorical metaphors, we at last reached the Promised Land.
And after 50 years following Brighton and Hove Albion I was there to witness the day, less than one mile from my home in Wolverhampton.

It was a lifetime since that first game at the Goldstone in September 1967, but for me, 14th April 2017 was the day the wheel had turned full circle.

Purists will tell me that the mathematical certainty of promotion to the Premier League wasn't assured until three days later when we beat Wigan Athletic 2-1 at the Amex, but for all those at Molineux on that grey Spring day in April this was the occasion when we achieved our dream.

The *"Sublime Day in May"* at St James Park in 1979 when we were first promoted to the old League Division One will always stay with me, but this day in 2017 was something superior.

Maybe it was because we had waited 34 years for redemption, maybe it was because we were so close to oblivion on that day in Hereford in 1997, maybe it was because we had all been to the countless wet and miserable away days in places like Halifax, Luton and Grimsby, or maybe it was because I was now a 61-year-old grandfather and had a wife that loved coming to football matches… but this yes, day was different.

Supreme, sublime and divine.

Wolverhampton is as different from Brighton and Hove as you can possibly get. No seafront lawns or promenade, no piers, no North Laine – not even any Lanes – no bistros, pavement cafes or bijou craft ale houses or boutiques, no bohemian gay quarter, no street artists, no candy floss and no wine bars.

The heart of Wolverhampton city centre is Queen's Square

It is a post-industrial working city – like many others in the Midlands and the north of England - still struggling to survive on the remnants of its past. Dereliction, social poverty and decay are everywhere. The legacy of Margaret Thatcher's destruction of British manufacturing industry in the 1980s is obvious on almost every street corner.

Once famous for its woollen trade, Sunbeam motor cars, its Chubb locks, Viking, Marston, Star, Wulfruna and Rudge bicycles and pop groups Slade, Dexys Midnight Runners and singer Beverley Knight, little remains of its Black Country past, except the Banks's Brewery and its football team: three-times First Division champions and four times FA Cup winners Wolverhampton Wanderers.

And its people.

It took me a couple of years to adjust to living in Wolverhampton, but its cultural diversity and its people make it the most welcoming place I have ever lived.

At the last census, Wolverhampton had a population of 260,000. Of that population, 68% were declared as White, 17.5% South Asian, 6.9% Black and 5.1% Mixed Race. The city is recognised as one of the best examples of multiculturalism in England and racial tensions are among the lowest in the UK.

It was the bed of much Afro Caribbean immigration in the 1950s. This was followed by immigration from Pakistan and India in the 1960s and 1970s. Now decades later, those with black, brown and coffee-coloured skin mix, work, play and marry those with white and other coloured skin.

There are 22,000 Sikhs, 11,000 Muslims and 7,000 Hindus in Wolverhampton. But there is no racial or religious tension.

Within a mile radius of my house there is a Hindu temple, a Buddhist temple, two Sikh temples, a central Mosque and at least seven Christian churches of various denominations.

Most of those with Asian or African ancestry are now third or even fourth generation immigrants and speak English as their first language, often with a thick Wolves' accent that Noddy Holder would recognise as his own.

But I am not pretending it has always been like this.

201

I live in the parliamentary constituency which was once the seat of overt Conservative racist MP Enoch Powell, and there has been a later history in the 1980s of National Front and BNP activity in the area. But most inhabitants of Wolverhampton realise that under the skin we are all the same… we are all human beings struggling to make a living and make sense of our lives.

However, it is not all sunshine and light. Football is also a religion in the city and its ugly side sometimes pervades.

Just two years prior to our game in 2017, three teenage Wolves supporters were jailed after they launched a unprovoked assault on a 44-year-old Watford fan after a home game, leaving him with a life-changing brain injury.

Yes, that's me, watching the end of season game against Middlesbrough in *The Hogshead* in May 2016

And in January of 2017 a local derby with Aston Villa was marred by violence and damage to the away end toilets at Molineux and property in the town. The statue to England legend Billy Wright was also damaged after a drunk driver crashed his car into its plinth after post-match revelry.

Hence almost every pub in the city has a "home fans only" rule, with heavy bouncers stationed at each doorway.

The Hogshead in Stafford Street in the city centre is a wonderful, large and welcoming watering hole with an array of beers and food and live football on at least four giant screens. It embodies friendliness and at the end of the 2015/16 season I even mixed with Wolves fans and shared beers to watch our end of season game at Middlesbrough live on TV, the game where Dale Stephens was controversially sent off, marring our chances of automatic promotion. Even Wolves' fans next to me shouted: *"That was never a red card!"*

But on match days, away fans have to make other plans if they want convivial refreshments.

So in April 2017 I wondered if I could do something small to change that city centre tradition. About a week before our game I talked about our dichotomy with a good friend and fellow socialist activist named Em.

"I am sure my local can oblige," she replied cheerily, with a broad smile. Em in turn spoke to the landlord of **The Combermere Arms** – a small and traditional pub - almost next door to the Banks's Brewery at Chapel Ash, and he confirmed he would welcome Albion fans in their club colours at his hostelry for the duration of the day.

And through the wonders of social media the message was quickly spread around.

On the day itself, Gill and I walked the short distance from our home at about 1pm, to find the Combermere mobbed by scores of Albion fans decked out in blue and white stripes, sharing beers and banter with Wolves supporters – many in family groups. The bonhomie was tangible and good natured as we drank and chatted for the next hour.

Then sometime before 2.30pm we strolled as a group of about a dozen fans via Bath Road the half a mile to Molineux stadium.

Albion supporters leave *The Combermere Arms* **at Chapel Ash on our way to the game**

As we made our way smiles were shared with Wolves fans all en-route to the game. A big crowd was gathering as we made our way through the turnstiles in the Steve Bull stand – an older stand which runs the entire length of the south side of the ground.

I had attended the corresponding fixture the previous season (a 0-0 draw marred by Tomer Hemed missing a penalty) when we had only filled a third of the lower section of the stand. But this time we had sold out with more than 3,500 Brighton and Hove Albion fans (out of an attendance of 23,221) filling the entire lower section of the stand.

Albion fans fill the lower section of the famous Steve Bull stand

Before kick-off we sat top of the table on 86 points from 41 games, two points ahead of Newcastle United, and more importantly 12 points and a 30 plus goal difference ahead of Huddersfield Town in third place.

We all knew that a victory that day, with only four games remaining, would seal promotion, bar a mathematical disaster.

Our team that day had a promotion feel about it, even if it wasn't totally our first XI. David Stockdale in goal – who had enjoyed an amazing season – was behind a defence of Bruno, the BFG Hunemeier, Lewis Dunk and Pocognoli, a midfield of Knockaert, Stephens, Sidwell and March, with Glenn Murray and Hemed up top.

The Steve Bull stand was buzzing and the chants of *"We are going up"* and *"We're on our way to the Premier League"* didn't stop for a whole 90 minutes.

Although the Wolves supporters were making their own noise, they could barely be heard above the incessant singing of our fans.

It was a party atmosphere from kick-off until the final whistle.

On the pitch, with rain starting to fall, the hosts started well enough but the Albion's superiority almost showed within 15 minutes when Saiss gifted Dale Stephens the ball and he found Knockaert.

The winger then fed Hemed and he struck the angle of post and bar with a thunderous drive. We all gasped and at that point collectively realised we could win this game with some room to spare.

Knockaert powers through to score his first goal of the game
© BHAFC/Paul Hazlewood

Wolves offered plenty of endeavour and pressed with enthusiasm but lacked the quality to unlock our midfield or defence. And we gradually took control with some well-rehearsed slick passing.

A stretching Hemed directed Bruno's cross off target on 25 minutes, while he also had a header tipped over by Andy Lonergan six minutes later.

The Albion eventually took the lead on the stroke of half-time after a defensive nightmare from Wolves.

There seemed little danger when David Stockdale launched a long clearance downfield but defender Hause completely mis-read the flight of the ball, letting Knockaert in.

The 25-year-old raced towards the area and, despite Hause's desperate attempts to recover, he embarrassed Lonergan as his near-post effort went through the Wolves keeper's attempted save.

In the stand chants of *"We've got Knockaert, Anthony Knockaert"* took over from the continuous promotion songs.

Next to me, my wife was trying to restrain my excitement – but to little avail!

On the pitch it was also pandemonium as Knockaert almost leapt the perimeter fence to celebrate with family members away to our right.

Hemed then shot over as Albion went for the kill before the break and the Israeli striker continued to torment Wolves, diverting a cross over five minutes after the restart.

Wolves struggled to find a way back but did finally force Stockdale into action after an hour when he saved smartly from Conor Coady's header.

Ben Marshall prodded straight at Stockdale with 18 minutes left and then saw the goalkeeper beat away his angled drive as the plucky, yet limited Wolves tried to increase the pressure on Brighton.

But we made the game safe with eight minutes to play when Knockaert grabbed his second, squeezing the ball under Lonergan after a quick break.

On the final whistle, with some restrained celebration (clearly under instructions that promotion was not mathematically sealed) the players ran to the Steve Bull stand to suck in the delirium of their fans.

We stood top of the table on 89 points from 42 games, still four points ahead of Newcastle United and 12 points ahead of Huddersfield in third place, but with a 31 goal superior goal difference.

We knew that we would be mathematically promoted to the Premier

League on Monday if we beat Wigan and Huddersfield fail to beat Derby. For us all, we were there already there.

And as we danced, chanted and sang our way out of the stadium, past smiling police officers and glum Wolves fans, football was at last coming home.

Gill and I made our way to *Slaters* – the only place resembling a wine bar in the city centre – and past two mean looking bouncers, who greeted us with smiles, to savour some celebratory glasses of champagne.

Some three years after her first Albion game at Port Vale, my wife was at last drinking champagne at a football match.

And after 34 years in the wilderness – and 50 years since my first game - football was at last coming home!

It had been some journey.

Brighton and Hove Albion finished the 2016-17 season as runners-up in the Championship with 93 points, just one point behind champions Newcastle United, and eight points ahead of third placed Reading. Only a disappointing final three games snatched the title away from us. But we were promoted to the top flight for the first time since 1983.

Who Ate All the Pies? Wolves

The Banks's Park Brewery is half a mile from Molineux and dominates the Chapel Ash roundabout.
Pork Scratchings are the Black Country's answer to crisps and are much softer than the hard rind scratchings found in Yorkshire and Lancashire. They are often eaten with a sprinkling of Worcestershire Sauce and washed down with Banks's Amber, Mild or Bitter beer. Bostin' Cracklin' is made less than half a mile from my home!

About the Author

Death in Grimsby is written and edited by Nic Outterside, and published by **Time is an Ocean Publications**.
Nic is a lifelong Brighton and Hove Albion fan, an award-winning journalist and creative author, who over 34 years has worked across all forms of media, including radio, magazines, newspapers, books and online.
Among more than a dozen awards to his name are *North of England Daily Journalist of the Year, Scottish Daily Journalist of the Year, Scottish Weekly*

Journalist of the Year and a special award for investigative journalism. In 2004 Nic was named BBC Radio Five Live's Football Fan of the Year. In 2016 Nic was awarded an honorary doctorate in written journalism. *Death in Grimsby* is his seventh published paperback book.

BOOKS
Author and Editor:
The Hill - Songs and Poems of Darkness and Light
Another Hill - Songs and Poems of Love and Theft
Luminance - Words for a World Gone Wrong
Blood in the Cracks
Asian Voices
Death in Grimsby

Picture Credits

Page 118	BHAFC
Page 121	Ian Hine/Seagulls Programmes
Page 123	BHAFC
Page 126	BHAFC
Page 128	Nigel Hardy
Page 165	The Argus
Page 187	The Sentinel
Page 194	BHAFC/Paul Hazlewood
Page 206	BHAFC/Paul Hazlewood

Thanks also for help in providing products or locations for some of the food and drink photographs:
Bulmers Cider, Hereford
The Village Bakery, Coedpoeth
The Ludlow Brewing Company, Ludlow
Purcells' Butchers, Whitchurch, Shropshire
Banks's Brewery, Wolverhampton
Gill's Pork Products, Wolverhampton
FJ Tye & Sons, Wolverhampton
The Starting Gate Ale House, Wolverhampton

Bibliography

Jonathan Livingstone Seagull – Richard Bach (1972)
ISBN 978-0-00-649034-0
Shoeless Joe – WP Kinsella (1982)
ISBN 0978-0-395-95773-7
Fever Pitch – Nick Hornby (1992)
ISBN 978-0-575-05910-9
Build a Bonfire – Stephen North & Paul Hodson (1997)
ISBN 978-1-90715-815-5
Park Life – Nick Varley (1999)
ISBN 978-0-14-027828-X
His Way – Patrick Murphy (2004)
ISBN 978-1-86105-849-2
Match of My Life – Paul Camillin (2009)
ISBN 978-1-84818-000-0
We Want Falmer – Steve North & Paul Hodson (2011)
ISBN 978-1-90715-816-2
Mad Man – Dick Knight (2013)
ISBN 978-1-907-637582
Football History Told Through Newspaper Headlines (2016)
ISBN 978-1-906688-66-0
Brighton & Hove Albion – JJ Waller (2017)
ISBN 978-0-957-439047
Bloody Southerners – Spencer Vignes (2018)
ISBN 978-1-785-90436-3

Afterword

For most birds flying is just a means of finding food, but for a Seagull, flying is life itself.
Jonathan Livingstone Seagull

It's our sacrosanct home, isn't it? You expect your aunty, your gran or grandad to die, but you never expect your football club.
Build a Bonfire

I won't miss Withdean – The Theatre of Trees. I remember playing Millwall there, we got absolutely drenched; we might as well have just jumped in a pool.
We Want Falmer

After living in the city for almost a decade I still didn't realise what it meant – I am truly overwhelmed.
Glenn Murray

It used to be a tenner for the day and non-stop singing, supporting players as ordinary as the fans standing watching them.
Park Life

The beauty of football isn't just the 90 minutes you see – it is the social side of it. It's your family, it's your friends.
Roy Chuter

While the details here are unique to me, I hope they will strike a chords with anyone who has found themselves drifting off, in the middle of a working day to a left-foot volley into the top right-hand corner, 10 or 15 or 25 years ago.
Nick Hornby

We shouldn't forget our history and we must remember how much a part the fans played.
Paul Samrah

The game ends and the players begin to drift off toward their exit, but the dreams and the memories will never end.
Shoeless Joe

Printed in Great Britain
by Amazon